FACING UP TO FATHER

Heath End Farm
VERNON JAMES MURRELL

Facing up to
FATHER

The pleasures and pains
of a Cotswold childhood

David Worlock

with illustrations *by* Rufus Mills

MARBLE HILL ᵛᵛ LONDON

First published in a limited Collector's Edition in 2020 by
Marble Hill Publishers Ltd
Flat 58 Macready House
75 Crawford Street
London W1H 5LP
www.marblehillpublishers.co.uk

This paperback edition first published in 2021

A CIP catalogue record for this book is
available from the British Library.

ISBN 978 1 8383036 2 4

Typset in Bell, Bodoni and Albertus

Printed and bound by Ingram Spark

Design by Dan Brown

To my three wonderful children,

KATE, LUCY & CHARLIE

Contents

Acknowledgements

THE READER who reaches the end of this book will readily determine that the real heroine rarely, and then only fleetingly, appears centre stage. Yet without the managerial skills and iron sense of purpose of my mother, we would none of us have survived childhood with Father. The intensity of her ambition for me and the sustaining love that she always directed at me were the countervailing forces. Despite struggles and the darker moments my childhood was a happy one, and it is because of her that I remember it so.

My story makes it clear that my three sisters played a vital role. They have been lifelong companions and best friends, and until pandemics intervened our annual gatherings, complete with children and grandchildren, were a highlight. Unsurprisingly, each of us has different memories of those years, but their kindness and encouragement in getting my version down has been immensely valuable to me. Needless to say, they are not responsible for the bits I got wrong.

It will also be clear that when the breaking-point came and I determined that I had to go to university, I found school-teachers prepared to help and support me, just as they had been partly responsible for awakening my educational appetites in the first place.

P. J. C. Despres was an inspired English teacher who remains in my ear whenever I read a new poem or an unfamiliar novel. Noel W. Johnston made me Secretary of the school library committee, my first responsible role in life, and awakened a lifelong interest in the American Civil War. Barry Sutton encouraged me to read in depth behind my history syllabus in a way not permitted by more modern examination systems. Above all, the Rev T. E. Warner, the school chaplain, recognised a struggling atheist and turned on me the full force of his confidence and enthusiasm. With allies like this, how could I fail? Or how could I fail the expectations that people like this had of me? These men remain for me the quintessence of education: teachers who struggle to help you to find yourself in life and equip you with the critical tools for living it. I owe them so much and I am dismally aware of how pathetic were my efforts to tell them this.

I owe special gratitude to my sister Mo and her son Rufus Mills for permission to use the sketch of Heath End Farm by her first husband and Rufus's father, the late Vernon James Murrell. Jim Murrell was a distinguished restorer of miniatures at the Victoria and Albert Museum as well as a considerable artist and illustrator in his own right. I am therefore doubly grateful to his son, Rufus, who accepted the invitation to contribute the chapter opening sketches.

I owe a great and real debt to my publisher. I had the good fortune to work with Francis Bennett on the foundations of his company, Book Data. History will see him as a key figure in creating the information needed to allow books to survive successfully in a digital age. The same galvanic energy and undimmed enthusiasm has carried me from a tentative writer to publication, aided hugely by the editorial efforts of Tessa, his wife. Grateful as I am, I am proud that these two are my friends. I am grateful as well for the work of Dan Brown: not solely a designer but a thoughtful and forensic reader. Once again, however, all remaining lapses remain the fault of the author.

This book would never have been written without the intervention of one person. Her tactful questions about my early life, her interest as a trained psychotherapist in what I thought the motivations of the characters in this story might be, and above all her loving support when I flagged and doubted, made my wife, Anne, central to this effort. My love and gratitude has no bounds.

DAVID WORLOCK

Speen, Bucks
August 2020

"History is a speculative discipline."

WILLIAM GIBSON

Financial Times
15 February 2020

Preface

HOW WELL DID YOU know your paternal grandfather? When I mentally address this question to each of my three children I realise that each of us has a slightly different perspective, which is natural, as well as memories and blanks. Kate had the joy of her grandfather's teasing old age, all soft edges and eccentric touches. Lucy was cradled in the gnarled old arms, like being rocked in some ancient tree. And Charlie has nothing, just like me. My paternal grandfather died of the Spanish flu in 1918. I have spent a lifetime wondering about him. All the witnesses I quizzed while they were alive were equivocal or contradictory, and now they too are all dead.

So I shall try to leave you a faded garland of memories by which to form views of your own. I suspect that you will not find a clear and unequivocal answer here, but some strong emotions spun across time. In the fifty or more years of our relationship my father and I ran through the full gamut of human regard. Please form your own views. I am an unreliable narrator, in both the literal and the literary sense. In my half-remembered truths others will find distortion, fiction in my faction. Try to look beyond and understand us both, Father and I, trapped in strong emotions, stirring times, and constant change, each trying to recognise each other for what we really are and mean.

Chapter 1

Into the Garden

S O LET'S GET STARTED. Join me outside of the front door of Nibley Farm. This is a not very distinguished early Jacobean E-shaped farmhouse in South Gloucestershire, its wings enclosing a tiny paved courtyard. The front range of the house is very plain, distinguished by the door before which we now stand. A huge, brown-varnished, oak-panelled door, crossgartered with great black metal struts and hinges, is set in an arched surround with an oddly ecclesiastical feel about it. We will go beyond it shortly but first look in front. Neat lawns run down a slope to the gate opening onto the main road. On the other side of the road you can see the Swan Inn, where either Old or Young Dick Griffith greet their customers.

Between us a tall privet hedge, and an ever busier main road carrying heavy traffic from Chipping Sodbury, our nearest town, to Bristol, thirteen miles away to the south. To complete the geography, I should say that we are at a crossroads, the north side of the house being bounded by Nibley Lane, leading to Westerleigh and Wapley. On the other side of the main road, which is steadily leaching away at our front garden through council road widening and visibility schemes, Nibley Lane runs on, over the Nibley brook and past the mill to the unknown splendours and mysteries that are Iron Acton.

But we have not come to the front door solely for a geography lesson. Let's move to the extensive gardens on the south side of the house. Two large lawns, raised up a few feet as if on a parterre, are bounded at the far end by a door and a high wall, screening this private pleasure quarter from the noisy life of the farmyards beyond. The high wall curls to enfold a summer house mostly used as a tool shed and then a dark but wonderfully secluded stone hut with a very gothic slit window, the outside privy. Thoughtfully provided with back numbers of *Farmers Weekly* (we had to give up *Farmer and Stockbreeder* when its new shiny paper stock proved too rough for comfort for those brought up on newsprint), it is both a hiding place for those pursued by chores and duties and a place of philosophical contemplation for those struggling on the nursery slopes of stoicism. It also links to one of the themes of childhood since, after godliness, my mother's greatest ambition for her children is regularity. The answer, in a large, old farmhouse with only one inside toilet, is often this: "Outside". It is the same answer we give when Father is not available to answer the phone. We all know what it means, and that it could be a long wait.

Digression is all very well in the picaresque, but it defeats our gardening objectives. I need to make some introductions.

Two people are kneeling on the lawn on small rubber mats. At first sight a religious ritual might be taking place. Each of the worshippers is armed with metal shears, agricultural legacies of sheep shearing. The one in front is my mother. The one behind her on the other side of the newly mown lawns is my sister Jane, aged about 18. They are "cutting round", clipping away excess grass from the edge of the lawn. It is a ritual. Nothing is finished until it is done. We all get to do it, though there are two notable absentees from the clipping squad today. If you listen carefully for a moment you might just hear their giggles and squeals from beyond the garden wall. These noises are coming from the stables. My two other sisters are excused cutting-round duties since they are needed for "higher purposes". With hot water and saddle soap they are cleaning tack. For tomorrow Father will be with His Grace in Wednesday Country.

But where is this Father? Let's go past the clipping worshippers, past the rosebushes in glorious bloom, beyond the flower gardens which are my mother's joy and which decorate her house, and meet a red-faced perspiring figure planting shallots. Alongside these he has onions. His King Edwards are banked in rows. Beans and peas gracefully climb their poles behind the banked asparagus rows, coated and clothed in layers of soot and horse manure. Raspberry canes, strawberry beds and gooseberry bushes cluster around the outside privy, grateful beneficiaries of its inefficient soakaway. A line of tall terracotta pots march like grenadiers beside the path, each treasuring in its heart of darkness forced rhubarb which will only catch a glimmering light when the gardener removes the lids to irrigate them with his own special internally distilled growing mixture, usually applied last thing at night.

We came here to meet my father, and here he is in guise of gardener, the man who as a boy won the gardener's cup at school and sold vegetables to the masters' wives. We find a perspiring man, with a red knotted handkerchief on his head, broad braces straining around an ample girth, a slightly jowly red face marked by the great, hooked Worlock–Hatherall nose he has inherited from his forebears. These are the lived-in features of a working farmer at this time in his late forties. Survival has been a struggle in a family history, as we shall see, with plenty of failure to talk about. It is around 1955. Farming is looking better than in his previous three decades. When he is not being rescued from ridiculous depths of near-terminal pessimism by my mother, he can soar like a Quixote into a world where everything is possible and he can do it. Look carefully at the perspiring garden labourer: tomorrow morning we shall meet the mounted hunting farmer, astride the eighteen-hand bay gelding, saddlery gleaming, hip flasks of port and brandy and some rich fruit cake stowed on board. A new day. A different person.

IN THE CHAPTERS that follow we shall pursue the many faces of Father, and catch at any pale reflections of his own father, my grandfather, that we can trap down in the process. Both men were reckless risk-takers, according to my grandmother. Neither had a good head for strong liquor, though both loved a drink. Both of them felt better on a horse than walking at street level. Neither of them were natural businessmen. Both, it was often said, could be plunged into deep and hopeless depression, from which they could only be roused by the strong, combative women they had married. Both were subject to rapid changes of mood. Both appreciated domestic life and children – but on their terms, when they were ready. Both nursed great expectations for their children. Neither felt an involvement in

4

their children's upbringing: this was a woman's work. They were not "modern" men.

Much of this was already clear to me in 1955, either by listening to family talk, or in that covert, near sub-conscious way that knowledge is transmitted in families. So I did not expect Father to play with me and my train set. I would have been surprised if he had ever mentioned that he knew that I had one. His role was to engage with the great outdoors successfully enough for his wife and four children to be fed, clothed and educated. He knew that if he accomplished this he was beyond criticism. Family conversation in 1955 was still very likely to hark back to the pre-war history of agricultural depression. Hard times cast long shadows. The adults around the dinner tables of my childhood knew enough about failure, examples of the consequences of failure, and the the paralysing effects of fear of failure to write a manual on the subject, and it was a subject that did not weary them in repetition.

At the heart of these discussions lay two parallel concerns. One was continuity. Farming was not done piecemeal. As soon as a crop was harvested a new one had to be planned and planted. As soon as the steers went to market the grass they had grazed must be grazed by their successors. Milking, the cash flow necessity of daily life, took place morning and evening, but only because of the husbandry which kept cows in the cycle of producing calves and thus milk. This continuum did not stop for the normal offices of other people's lives. I early learnt that farmers did not get sick, did not take family holidays and did not retire. But they were allowed to die, and when that happened they should have a male heir ready to take over. A woman could be a farmer, as my grandmother had shown, but it took a very rare woman. Farmers in my childhood were as anxious for a male heir as any Tudor monarch securing dynastic succession. I was the youngest of four children, my three elder siblings all being girls. And, as we shall see, farmers had a very Hanoverian tendency to quarrel with the succession: memories of Young Farmers meetings were littered with anecdotes of dogmatic farmer fathers in dispute with their more progressive sons during an apprenticeship to succession which could last forty years.

Father knew all about continuity and succession. He had succeeded to the farming role at age ten when the Spanish flu pandemic robbed him of a 39-year-old father, a mentor he already found difficult and dictatorial. A generation later I would soon be wondering, with the arrogance of childhood, whether I wanted to become a farmer. The very thought that I might think that a choice was involved had never occurred to Father. This set the stage for a decade of dispute, followed by a long journey of reconciliation. A voyage of discovery for both of us.

Chapter 2

Onto the Tump

B UT DELICIOUS THOUGH IT IS in the early evening in the vegetable garden, we must move on. Move past the gardening farmer and see the ivy-covered crumbling wall that in turn bounds the garden on its southern side. A rusty metal gate in this wall allows us into the field beyond, but pause before opening it. All is silent, but we are being watched by over a hundred intense little eyes. You can almost hear the pent-up breath behind those eyes. Yet nothing stirs. The Tump, a paddock completely covered with docks and horseradish chest-high to a nine-year-old, is a Mato Grosso, an equatorial jungle so far unexplored but not uninhabited. As we lift the latch on the gate, fifty little piglets flee in panic, shaking the tropical forest cover like a typhoon. They coalesce again as a tribe further down the hill that gives the Tump its name, behind the defensive line of deep mud baths which their mothers have hollowed out, and from which those beldames are now arising to see who dares to interrupt their luxurious ablutions.

This is our piggery. At night its denizens are secured in a thatched shed and several sties on our left. There too is the gateway that takes us out of the Tump into the main farmyards. Stand by that gate a moment. The mothers have decided we are no threat and have sunk back into their muddy bath water. The offspring have resumed the chasing games that have created tiny pig paths through the jungles. In the restless life of the farm this is a very tranquil place, but it is not always so. Here, in this very gateway, we have played games of a very different sort.

"Bring two pieces of corrugated iron," says Father.

Easy enough, for there is a huge pile of corrugated iron sheets beside the yard gate. It comes from roofs or the sides of sheds. Father never throws anything away: we just pile it somewhere, believing in his utter faith that, whatever the rusting object is, it will "come in" some day. And truly we do use the corrugated: to fence livestock in, to temporarily (i.e. permanently) block a hole to stop animals getting out or, as now, to form a temporary pen. The sheets will make an enclosure bounded by the Tump gate, the sty wall and the garden wall. The Tump gate is pig-proof with chicken wire. Father steps into the arena we have created and I see he is well prepared. He tucks into a niche in the wall two Gillette razor blades and a two-inch darning needle trailing a length of coarse cotton.

Father is in a benign mood. It is a Sunday morning and we both pause to take in the church bells. Now Iron Acton, now Westerleigh, now Wapley.

A joke is proposed: "This is going to get fairly noisy, so pay no mind. But if it gets noisy enough it may put Reverend Wynne off his sermon, just like the Russians jamming the Yanks' radio station in Munich."

The reference to Radio Free Europe is topical and he knows that I have become an avid reader of newspaper headlines in the *News Chronicle*. The reference to the incumbent at Wapley brings in a local hate figure, infamous for demolishing Worlock gravestones and laying them in the vicarage garden path. Old John Worlock of Culverhill and his sons had been up there recently and took their tombstones away at dead of night in a Land Rover. We are spoiling for a fight, and Father is working up a mood.

But now the action centres on me. In the sty are some two litters, fifteen or so piglets, who will shortly be ready to join their older colleagues on the joyful Tump. But first they must be castrated, to ensure quick growth on low inputs. This is a cash crop, out the door within weeks, renewed three months three weeks and three days later by a new yield of piglets. We don't waste much time on them. Let's get this Sunday morning task done quick.

"Catch me a pig, boy!"

I go into the sty and bring out as many as I can in one go. Easy at first to grab one.

"Hold him by his hind legs, boy! Wider!"

Father feels for a testicle. The blade makes a cut, out pops a round, brown artefact, the blade severs it from its rightful owner, and it falls into the mud. Other pigs, even the dog until driven off with kicks and oaths, will fight to eat these trophies. Now the other side. Holding the wriggling animal drains strength quickly, the noise makes speech only intermittently possible, but the cut piglet is dumped unceremoniously over the Tump gate and it is time to find another, and another.

Father wants to go faster at about the same rate as I grow tired, and it gets harder to tackle and catch piglets as they get fewer and have more space in which to evade me.

And so the cursing begins. At first it is just my general uselessness, total inability to concentrate, and cack-handedness which are called to account. Then we have a piglet that, once restored to the floor, empties its intestines out of the castration cuts. This one has to be retrieved, though it moves deceptively fast, its guts stuffed back in with Father's horny forefinger and then sewn up with the darning needle. But it all wastes time, compounded by me knocking over one of the corrugated-iron sheets. A piglet makes a break for freedom. My rugby tackle brings him down across the yard by the cow-manure heaps, but when I bring him back the cursing has taken a darker turn.

At last we are done. We are both coated with mud and pig blood. Father collects up his tools, motions me to return the corrugated-iron sheets to the pile, and I receive a parting blessing:

"You know that you are useless, that you never will be any good, that I might as well not have a son as one who cannot get anything right. Now go to your mother and get cleaned up."

And so things are left at a point of disappointment, of inadequacy, of an underlying conviction that whatever efforts are made, adequacy can never be achieved, and not just on this day. Piglets are castrated every month, though the human cast varies with availability. Everyone working on the farm knows the fragile temper. Everyone has been "cussed to kingdom come and back" as our expression has it.

"Just try to ignore him," counsel my sisters. But neither they nor I can entirely accomplish this when the anger flows from Father on his horse, supervising us herding yearling heifers back from pasture through the housing estates of Yate, trying to prevent the flighty creatures from raiding every garden en route. Tears flow on all sides, our uselessness individually and as a family is fully explored. Nobby, younger brother of Bob Williams, our senior farmhand, says Bob has told Father he will not work with him when he gets like this. I know I am not the only one, but I am the only son.

Father never in his life tries to strike me. As the years pass I come to recognise that much of what he shouts at me matches what was shouted at him when he was a boy before the age of ten. I come to understand so many things when I finally understand that not only could he not please his own father, but his own father then died.

But for now a childish but firm resolve is building up in me: I will do everything I can to avoid working with him and will seek every means of expressing myself in non-agricultural contexts that I can find.

Chapter 3

Father Builder

Now we have met one face of Father, a terrible one, and, as we shall see, a recurrent one. But there are others, many others, and they can be quickly brought into play as moods change and, to the bewilderment of his family, moods can change in a moment.

On this Sunday afternoon when I am nine, Father has turned to a pet passion. At the back of the farmhouse is an old woodshed, and in front of it a little yard covered in shavings where kindling and timber is cut for the house fires. My mother does not wish to view this semi-industrial wasteland from her kitchen window. At this moment she can only see part of it, since the view is curtailed and the kitchen made dark by the wall that screens the little courtyard at the back of the house.

Doing something for our mother strikes a bell with everyone. Father is a very devoted and reliant husband. He conceives a plan for knocking down the curtain wall and letting light and air into the kitchen windows and the washing feebly waving on the lines in front of them. But one idea is not enough. This Father is a serial ideas man, and when possessed cannot be held back. My mother is wrong: it is not that he does not know when to stop. He cannot stop. No sooner has the wall disappeared than a rockery begins to rise in its place, built in local Yate-red spar stone. One tug of the woodstore and it falls over, but when foundations go in they reveal an unfamiliar curved wall structure. We are building a summer tea-house on the yet-to-be-planted lawn. It will be thatched, but not just with straw but with reeds from the Somerset levels. How do we separate the tea drinkers from the *hoi polloi* who use the gravelled farmyard beyond it? Why not a fifty-foot-long raised flower bed with stone walls either side constructed in Cornish herring-bone fashion?

Walls have to be built at speed, but they can only be built by the Master Builder. Each stone had to fit its neighbour. Anyone observing who helpfully suggested cement was solemnly cursed as a simpleton who would soon join his forebears roasting in the lower chambers of eternal fire. Walls were meant to be drystone, as any Cotswold man knew. There could be no exceptions, though in retrospect I know of one. The little courtyard, now full of light, had three steps up before you left it through an entrance flanked by two stone pillars. Now revealed, they looked odd. Father saw them as an opportunity. He would create a stone arch to span them. We searched for a great flat stone of three feet in length to do the job. None was available. Then inspiration struck: we would jam in an arch of Cotswold "toppers".

Father was not an engineer. In fact the very opposite. On the top of our Cotswold drystone walls we placed a vertical layer of large stones, jammed together upright. This gave weight and solidity to keep everything in place below, while displaying the rough edges of the stones to stock who might be tempted to scramble over the top. A collection of these stones, jammed in with force in an arc shape, could stand of its own volition and provide the capstone, as it were, to the "improvements" that had arisen when my mother remarked how dark the kitchen was and how other farmers' wives did not have a wood yard at their back door. We recall that socially rising yeoman farmers must beautify the premises. It is a hidden driver in much that follows.

So first we begin with the objective testing of theory. Father selects the required toppers. He climbs to the top of the ladder. Holding the first stones in place he accepts fresh stones from me and from Gerald Prendergast, newly returned to the village from National Service in Cyprus and now a trainee farmhand. Tension mounts until the builder's strength fails, he cannot hold the stones he has placed and place new ones, the ladder leans over at a crazy angle, stones crash down around Gerald and myself, and a moment of fear dissolves into a moment of Laurel and Hardy. But we have only just begun.

As we help the great builder to his feet, sympathise with his cuts and bruises, and ask if we can clear up the mess, it is plain that the iron has entered the soul of the arch constructor. He says he has just the thing put by for such a day as this and, after disappearing for ten minutes, re-emerges from the bottom of the yard with a piece of very thick gauge wire concrete reinforcement. This is bent into a neo-gothic arch shape and jammed between the tops of the pillars. Father and Gerald ascend on ladders on either side to jam in stones that I hand up from below. Twice more we stand admiringly below. Twice more there is a slip, a creak and a collapse. My mother's view is that it is a danger and she is scared for herself and her children to walk under it. Father is unmoved. We must try again. Let those afraid use the front door.

It is almost dark. The builders ascend the ladders. Stones are selected, rejected, then reselected for use elsewhere. Much manic determination is displayed, and at last it all stays in place. Job done. I show my mother that passage under the arch is really safe if you are running as fast as you can. Indoors my mother says she has something for Gerald's mother and can he wait on a moment. Father goes out to the horses. A few minutes later I am called outside to hold Gerald's ladder as he slaps half a bucket of cement on top of the arch. Nothing is ever said, and in the morning you cannot see it from below, though I note that my mother has washed the steps and there are no drips of drying cement in sight.

Did he know? I never asked. Twenty years later, when we had a completely different relationship, we often worked on walls and hedges together. Father held the theory that if he accepted the fact, by now many years apparent, that I was never going to return to run the family farm, then I had to accept learning vital life skills from him.

"Brainwork will let you down one day, Dave, but I can teach you two things that will keep you in employment all your days."

And so, in the farm at Evenlode (to which we moved in 1964 after my sisters had grown up and left home) we started on a tutelage that lasted my years at Cambridge and went on into the next decade.

Hedge laying and drystone walling, the golden arts to which he referred, are both intensely physical activities and I was glad

I was playing a good deal of rugby during these years. But they are also both thoughtfully intellectual activities. When hedge laying you must see the end result in its bushy beginnings. What to select as uprights to secure the fence, which elements can be half cut and bent down laterally, so as to grow out and form a sheep-proof, hole-free base, and which elements to dispense with altogether. Judicious choice lies at the heart of it. Similar strictures apply to drystone walling. This 3D jigsaw puzzle relies on locking the stones together across the wall as well as up and down. We worked on rockeries, a ha-ha and a flower bed shaped as a boat, but I never once handed him a stone for a slot without him pointing out that it needed another one jammed beneath or beside it. Having laid the hedges of the home paddock and then moved on to the home field and Yells Oziers, I at long last graduated as a practitioner. He was older by this time, and came out to watch me at work, sitting in the Land Rover with a flask, and then strolling over for an occasional inspection. I came to relish the pursed lips, the head shaking, and at length the grudging:

"If you must do it your way, I suppose that's half reasonable, but, mark me, you will have to do it all again in five years!"

Chapter 4

Yards and their Purposes

BUT WE MUST TRY to stay on track. The way to glimpse
the many personalities who combine to make up Father
is here, in the yards around the main farmyard. These
are years of change in agricultural practice. Over time the
supporting cast of workers diminishes: the five men are down
to one by the time we leave Nibley. The working horses have
been replaced by tractors. We have a stubby blue Fordson,
still bearing its Lend-Lease markers, and a larger and more
powerful red Nuffield. Father will use neither. Bob Williams
is king of tractors, he of the slicked Brylcream hair. I study his
rolling gait carefully. Do his hands actually touch the ground
when he turns corners?

Now that we have left the Tump we are in the wide expanse of the collecting yard. It slopes down from the back of the Great Barn. Once fully cobbled it now has patches of earth and grass in places. A complex of gates between the stables and the dairy is designed to admit vehicles, herds or flocks of various sizes. In this yard selection and collection takes place.

Livestock come to and from market. The wall of the cowshed, against which stands our extensive dungheaps, bounds one side of this rectangular space, while the other is marked by the stable and the boundary wall of the garden. I cannot see the space in my mind without envisaging the great Battle of Horncastle, and on this battlefield Father emerges as a Leader of Men.

Cows with horns had been a problem on British farms for years. Our wonderful Ayrshire Shorthorn herd was giving way to Friesians and a couple of Guernseys to give rich milk for the house, but everything still had horns. Cow carcasses diminished in value when the leather tanned from the hides was disfigured by cuts and scratches caused by constant inter-action with another cow's horns. Besides which, if you could feed ten young, horned beasts from a trough, then fourteen could dine in comfort in the same space without horns. The Ministry leaflet specified how dehorning was to be done, as well as indicating the acid preparation that was to be used to prevent the stumps regrowing, and applied to the crowns of calves to stop growth starting. If farmers were worried about doing this, they should consult their vet or invoke a vet-led Ministry team.

One thing Father was not was "worried". He grasped the point immediately. A De-Horning Day was announced. Each of our five worthy workers was encouraged to bring a friend and as many hacksaws and blades as could be sourced. The cattle crush, that engine of pipework for holding a cow still, was placed centrally. Cows were held around the back of the cowshed, brought forward for horn-shedding and then placed in the lower yard. The day began in an orderly manner. Father supervised the first cow in, Paul Benjamin (Benny, our cowman) removed the first horn. It took fifteen minutes. We had eighty cows and almost a hundred calves and sucklers.

After a while Father began to fret. It was all taking too long. Gerald, with me assisting, was assigned to the calves. They proved resistant, not just to being anointed but to the burning sensations once the treatment was applied. Soon we are in the midst of a bucking, rearing, kicking congregation of young animals whose normal quiescence around humans has completely disappeared. We beat a retreat back to the collecting yard.

When I first saw Breughel's *Slaughter of the Innocents* I knew that I had been there before. Father's impatience with the speed of the work had overflowed into frustration. One band of Herod's soldiers was using a gate to hold a cow against the wall, while another hacked at her horns. A third group was holding an animal in place with iron bars, while the man with the saw circled to avoid the kicks. Two men were now sawing at the crush. Herod himself danced between these groups, his eyes blazing with excitement as he demanded greater efforts. He was tireless. He was very muddy, but above all he bore the signs of the fact the Ministry neglected to impart. The lower levels of the horn are full of blood vessels. No one was ready for the fountains of blood that resulted. Herod and his butchers were red coated from head to foot. Father's brown smock was coated, but still he urged us on. The working day ended in darkness when Fred Timbrell was sent for cider. The drinkers imbibed silently, then stood in wonderment next day at the huge pile of horns at the edge of the yard.

Here was a rare face of leadership, fuelled perhaps by desperation that the job should be done in a day. But other pressure events did not produce the same quality. During haymaking, harvesting and threshing, tasks were assigned and the leader could be a grumbling absentee. But it would also be wrong to give an impression that life with Father was humourless. It was not. We found many things amusing. The men found Father's ability to smoke their cigarettes all day, without appearing ever to have a packet of his own to offer, wryly amusing. I was their runner, regularly crossing the main road to Mr Lemon's village shop to buy Woodbines, the working man's smoke of the day, as they ran out. The fact that Father carried no money, no wrist watch or wallet was an interesting perplexity. So how did he get through life? And what was in his pockets?

This was simple. In his pockets were a soiled, red, polka-dot handkerchief, a penknife and a length of binder twine. He thought he could tell the time by the state of the sky and the position of the sun, and according to him he was never wrong. This was helped by the fact that he neither made nor kept appointments, and he stated clearly that he never wished to be anywhere where he did not have credit, a statement that in later life was refined into the maxim "A day spent more than five miles from my front door is a day wasted."

If he was an intriguing, eccentric and sometimes amusing figure, as well as occasionally a terrible one, to the little community of the yards, there were also moments of high comedy. As we move from the collecting yard down to the lower yard, we cross the site of two of them, lodged in the consciousness like historic cinema comedy shorts. These jerky, sepia-tinged sequences became stories told often and relished for their comic value. Father is the prime mover in both, but never the object of the humour. The first, which occurs in front of the gate between these two yards, is stored in my mind on a film spool labelled "Chris Hawkins's Olympian Leap". The other member of the cast is a new arrival currently penned in the lower yard. Barney is a young, untried Aberdeen Angus bull. Our old bull, an ancient Ayrshire Shorthorn normally tethered to the massive elm that dominates one end of the Rickyard, is not only past it, but out of fashion. Now we want to sell our herd's progeny as beef stores, and Barney will soon ensure better market prices.

But how good is Barney? Chris is delegated to bring down some bulling heifers from the cowsheds. We plan to introduce these young ladies to their new beau and then admire a ravishing performance. The girls are duly introduced into the yard, but something is amiss. Our young Lothario is in retreat, and soon disappears altogether into a covered pen. This is not part of Father's plan. Muttering that he bought this sonofabitch from a normally reliable Irish dealer at Gloucester, he invites Chris, also recently returned from National Service in Cyprus, to prove himself as a stockman in the making by going into the pen and rousting Barney out and pointing him at his duties. Chris replies that if it was Georgios Grivas, Archbishop Makarios and the whole of EOKA in that pen he would be happy to oblige, but he was a bit unsure about young bulls. Father starts to tease with implications that the girls of Nicosia in the last two years had faced a similar threat from Chris that Barney now posed to the simpering heifers. Eventually he riles him to such an extent that the red-faced young man opens the gate and strides over to the pen. In a moment he too has gone.

In the same moment he reappears. He is running hard towards us. A few yards behind him comes Barney, head down, going harder … and gaining. We at the gate are paralysed. We cannot open the gate – the beast is too close and will gore Chris as he tries to slip through. If both of them come through, the bull will catch him in the collecting yard within six strides at most. So we cling to both ends of the gate and hold it shut. And Chris, dear happy-go-lucky Chris, takes it all in and makes a decision. Wearing army fatigues, and heavy ex-army boots, the flying figure reaches the gate and leaps. One hand on top of the five-bar gate permitted an athletic vault which the athlete could not have known he possessed. Only a heavy boot catching the top bar ruined the personal best and sent the athlete spiralling into the muck of the yard. We rush to sit beside him, to comfort his pride and his bruises and to point out the danger avoided. Father says he will send him to Pamplona and Chris thanks him, saying he has always fancied the Costa Brava. We conclude that Barney is gay and he goes back to Gloucester the following week with an even higher reputation than the Irishman gave him.

Father loved this story and even late in life I could make him laugh just by saying "do you remember the day Chris leapt the gate. The same is true of my second archival film loop, also enacted in that same lower yard. The label reads "The Day Dave Rode the Pig". As it opens we find a not unusually impatient Father with a small pig-related task in hand. He has a gilt, a biggish young lady just about to be put in with the mature sows to be served in turn by our hyperactive boar. But before all of these good things could come to pass she must have a ring put in her nose. This it is hoped will deter her from constant digging in the earth, though the heavily ringed sows out on the Tump already seem to act like pigs from Wimpey. But threats to the horseradish, inseparable from his beloved joint of topside, are a serious consideration for Father and the Tump's foliage cannot be endangered. So Father has assembled the things he needs to get this quick job done. First the pliers-like device with its grooved slot. Once the big brass open ring with its needle-sharp ends has been placed in the grooves it is the work of moments to clamp it into the pig's nostrils, penetrating the soft flesh until, hopefully, the two ends of the ring meet.

Some pigs are easy. This is not one of them. Father has tried surreptitious approaches. He has tried putting down food. He should put her in the cattle crush, but it is too far away, and he is too busy, and I am too handy.

"Do your feet touch the ground either side of her?" he asks.

I try. Just, on tip-toe.

"Right," says my instructor, "sit on her shoulders and hold her prick ears (she is a Large White) while I do this little job."

We both address the gilt at once. I grip, he grabs the nose, down come the pliers … and as they do so she bucks her head to be rid of us both. She is brilliantly successful. Her 45-year-old tormentor falls over in the yard. Her nine-year-old attacker is prone on her back, and she herself is shuttling backwards to shake him off. As he slides forward he sees that one end of the ring is firmly in her nose, but the other end sticks out from her nose at right angles.

As I watch the short movie in my mind's eye the denouement seems inevitable. The moment when the boy slips down the nose, but his Wellington snags on the outstretched arm of the ring, the moment when the point of the ring goes through the boot and deep into the leg within. To ease the pain the boy must climb back onto the animal. But the pig is strong. She starts to run. The boy is hoping his weight will tire her, but terror lends her strength. She runs past Father, sitting on the floor and laughing hysterically. (He is later to say that he had no idea I was attached to the pig, and not just riding it for pleasure.) Help arrives. The ring is removed from both participants. When the Wellington full of blood comes off there is a deep, long cut.

"Stitches?" says my mother.

"Bandages," says Father. "They are usually alive in the morning. But, Kath, you never saw anything as funny as that boy riding a pig round and round the yard…"

Chapter 5

The Disaster at Little Tump

I T IS SAD TO GUIDE YOU from the lower yard back into the collecting yard and then, by a sharp right turn along to the very small paddock we called the Little Tump. Sad because in retrospect it was here that people made determinations about the future that they should not have done, or at least in the course of twelve wet hours on a dour December day. To understand how this happened we need to be clear about the Little Tump as a *mise-en-scène*, and that the several years that have passed since the earlier episodes described above have wrought some changes. On my side, though I am earnestly assured by my mother and sisters that "it's just his way, he doesn't mean anything by it, he gets just as cross with us", I am beginning to believe Father. I am incompetent, I cannot get anything right, I will never function properly as a farmer's son. As my grandmother points out, Father's brother, my beloved Uncle Dick, has a son who can do everything on the farm, and he is only a year older than me. My conclusions are slow in forming through these years: I begin to resist, avoid and evade all efforts to get me to work on the farm directly alongside Father in circumstances where I will be cursed inevitably to "billybejazus", as his expression had it, and have my inadequacies in yet another important skills area fully exposed.

Father had changed too. He had seen what was happening, and fully realised my total reluctance to work anywhere near him. Always a bookish boy, I became more so, and while I enjoyed chores like feeding the four pigs in the sty near the farmhouse who were fed table scraps and were always named Tom, Dick, Harry and T'other, I would not work with Father. I was still fetching drinks and cigarettes for the men, and smoking them. I loved haymaking and harvest: when we worked in gangs, I rode the tractors with Bob Williams and felt no resentment when, while returning home one day on an empty trailer, one of its uprights shook loose and knocked me out as it fell. Even concussion could not convince me to work with Father.

But elsewhere the aspiration to make me the farmer's son that Father wanted, the succession the farm and family desperately needed, still burnt strongly. I heard the raised voices in the kitchen as my mother was berated by her mother-in-law.

"What do you mean, he won't work with his father? It's not his choice! You are turning him into a mummy's boy, Kath. Someone should show him some discipline."

So I was ready, on those days when my mother, centre of all things familial, came to me with the pleading voice.

"Your Father works so hard for all of us, Dave. He would be so pleased if you could just go out and ask if you could help. Tell him you want to work with him and learn."

I never resisted very long, and on the day of the Little Tump confrontation I was soon in front of Father's great chair in the living room.

"A job? The boy wants a job? Oh, yes, do I have a job for you!"

Father had indeed changed. He was no longer the despairing instructor in agricultural arts burdened with a mindless student. Now he would be the disciplinarian, instilling the obedience needed to create a useful member of the workforce. We trudge to the Little Tump and survey the scene. This tiny paddock used to have a brick calves' shed with a corrugated iron roof. The building had been deemed redundant earlier in the year and been demolished. I had helped take the roof away on the tractor. As we knocked down the walls some bricks had stayed stuck together with cement, but since Father wanted the bricks separated to form a building elsewhere, Gerald and I had gone to great pains to hammer them apart. Even so, we had not entirely succeeded. At the side of the paddock was a large stack of used bricks, higher and longer than I myself at that age, and beside it those remaining joined-up sections.

"Move all those bricks to the other side of the paddock."

"But what for?"

"None of your business to ask why. Just do it and let me not hear or see you until it is finished."

Flummoxed and flustered I begin the job, a brick in each hand. Then Gerald's cheerful face looms over the wall.

"What are you doing that for?"

"Who knows!"

He disappears, but is back a moment later with worn leather gauntlets, a bit big but welcome, and an inverted hemp feedbag to place on the back of my head as rain protection. Chris follows with the old blue sack trucks.

"Load the bigger bits on that and wheel them across," he sagely advises. Then both men stand a moment, watching the purposeless labours of a boy, and wondering at the eccentricities of Father.

The next face at the wall is Father's own. It is late morning. I am getting on better than I ever thought I would. At least two thirds of the bricks are moved. I want to report imminent success. Before I can check myself I sing out, "I shall be finished by lunchtime."

He departs without a word but I know that, for some reason, I have not pleased him. When he returns an hour later he is plainly very angry. This time I am more cautious and respectful.

"Can I go into lunch when I have finished?"

"You stupid little bugger, can't you see that *I* have to say when you have finished? And you will only have finished when you have moved every single damn brick back across the paddock and put it down exactly where you first found it this morning. And you will not leave this place until you have done so."

After he leaves I sit on the wall for a moment. The rain is lighter now but has still soaked me through. Then my sister Jane arrives. No one in the house knows what is happening, but she comes bearing a flask of hot soup. It seems to re-energise me. I know exactly what to do. Now I know what the job entails, I will finish it. Maybe this is what I am meant to learn, but I will not be told again that I am a failure. Maybe I will die or be mortally injured in the attempt, in which case they will be sorry and he will be blamed. As Jane returns to the house I set to work with a will.

I see her next a few hours later, as early winter dusk is falling. She brings two torches which she places on the wall. Although

I am wet to the skin, and shaking helplessly from the sustained effort, she does not try to persuade me to stop. Instead she sets about helping to move the remaining bricks. Then we go indoors. Hot bath, supper, bed. Very strangely, this episode is never mentioned again, not in my childhood, nor as an adult. In the different relationship forged with Father in later years it is never referenced.

Did I expect someone to say, "Well done, you finished the task"? Almost certainly not, for I had other learnings from the experience that took me in a different direction. The first was that my will was as strong as his. I would never work for him again in any context. I thought he was a complete fool and a figure of ridicule as the farm workers often portrayed him. Time would reveal how wrong I was; happy accidents brought us back together. But for now, I knew only that this farmer's son would never become a farmer. I accepted Father's definition of my future: if I was destined to be a useless failure then at least I would fail doing my own thing, and not this impossible farming business.

Chapter 6

Defending the Borders

P AUSE A MOMENT at the gateway between the Little Tump and the last of our yards, the Rickyard. As you lean with me on the gate, we are looking down a rough piece of pasture land sloping away from us to the sometimes trickling, sometimes somnolent Nibley Brook. The field is known as Stivvies, though it shows in the Land Registry as St Stephens. On the other side of a bridge of railway sleepers is a small conical hill, a spoil heap left over from the last century, from the Bristol coalfield, which once produced about 1% of British coal but is now defunct. The little hill is where I loved to play in my earliest years, and home of my imaginary pre-Disney animals, and in particular to Bill Badger, who always took my side against the outrageous oppressions of my middle sisters, whose great riding companionship and stable-based confederacy I very much envied. But, as they pointed out with pleasure, they are Older, and I am a Boy.

As we stand at the gate, I have grown beyond Bill, into double figures, and I am at an early stage in gaining some political consciousness. These are the deepest and darkest years of the Cold War. Father views the Russians with the utmost suspicion.

"Winnie was right – they were the real enemies all the time."

For me, the torch-in-bed bookworm reader already soaked deep in Rider Haggard and Capt W. E. Johns, this is confusing. I thought we had been fighting the Germans. And in my weekly copy of the *Eagle* we apparently still are.

These early thoughts on Friend and Foe are further confused by half a dozen yearling heifers despatched to the field just beyond Stivvies to see if they could find enough to eat in the green shoots coming up amongst the stubble. Whether they could or not remains an open question: they soon got bored trying. Their adolescent gaze was attracted by the lush pastures on the other side of the stream. The fence, on our side and our responsibility, needed repairing and was full of holes. The more obvious problems had been addressed by sheets of yet more corrugated iron. Father was a fitful repair man, sometimes seized with hedge-repair zeal, but often neglectful when other matters pressed. In this he was no different from most farmers we knew. The difference was that he was never Wrong.

The young beasts soon found a gap beyond the reach of corrugated iron. The brook's late summer trickle posed no problems. Soon they were grazing with equanimity on the very piece of quality grazing into which our next door neighbour, Tom Bennett, was, within a few days, about to introduce his milking herd. Tom's farm stretched south of ours, to the hamlet of Coalpit Heath. We had a mutual border along the brook. No part of this landscape remotely resembled Checkpoint Charlie and Coalpit Heath was no West Berlin.

It took a day or two for discovery and then tension to develop. We did not look at the heifers every day. Tom did not assess his grass keep until he needed it. But when he did, he rounded up our cattle, put them in a pen and sent his sons down to ask us to go up and bring them back. So far, nothing unusual. We knew the Bennett boys well. Peter was the same age as Jane, an outgoing and attractive young man and a pillar of the local Young Farmers. Sandy-haired Andrew was more reserved, three years older than me. We all subsequently went to the same school.

Father chose to return the visit alone on his horse. He went without a following of arm-waving, hollering, fleet-heeled children and dogs of his own, such as would normally be needed to herd heifers anywhere. It may have been the horse that was the critical negotiating failure. You really cannot have an equal conversation with someone sitting eighteen hands above you. Sitting up there can conjure illusions of power and authority in even the mildest of subjects. Father was not the mildest, and may have entered the discussion harbouring some residual feelings of guilt about the state of the fence.

Obviously we have no verbatim account of what took place. As we came to understand it a request to remove the strays was coupled with a request that the fence be secured to protect the Bennett herd from further incursions. The reply from the horse was haughty, it is said. The stock would be collected when the horseman was ready, but the fence served our purposes very well and would only be repaired when we needed to do so. The reply from ground level came hot and choleric. As long as the beasts were penned there they would not be fed, and they would not be released until the fence was made good, since who knew what disease risks the Worlock cattle might expose to the expensively inoculated Bennett herd. The man on the high horse drew himself higher. He was proud to say his farming was disease free, but just in case there was doubt he was prepared to leave his stock in quarantine in that pen, until starvation killed them if necessary, to see if disease broke out. But he did not propose ever to visit Seys Court Farm again or address its present occupants. On which note the horse turned and effected a dignified exit.

This year was my eleventh. One day I stood in the village shop deciding between a walnut whip and a liquorish twirl, and wondering why Gerald had changed from Woodbines to Park Drive cigarettes, when my eye was caught by the headlines on the twenty or so newspapers arranged on the table in front of me. They looked more like my comics than regular newspapers. British paras had invaded Egypt and seized the Suez Canal, in a secret pact with France and Israel. Every paper said the same: show them we cannot be pushed around, show them we are still an imperial power, might is right.

It grew worse. Father said we had to defend the passage to India and the East, that our money built the canal anyway, and that they were just Egyptians, Arabs who looked to us for civilised values. The irony of this never occurred to him, but then he never visited the Egyptian rooms of the British Museum. Gerald and Chris were no help; the paras were based in Cyprus. And to the farm community, the absolute right of the British to go round the world beating up anyone that they might describe as a wop or a wog or a "furriner" seemed an absolute given.

"Got to keep 'em in line, Dave," smiled my cousin Martin Raven, the ex-Royal Marine.

Only my mother's brother Don, by now a regional manager in Shell Mex and BP in Manchester, had a world view.

"It's all about the oil, Robs," he told his brother-in-law in the patronising tone that always infuriated Father. "If you have some stocks and shares, some savings, money that you use as a hedge against poor harvests, liquidate it now and buy shares in Ultramar oil from Mexico and Venezuela. As long as that canal is blocked and Middle East oil cannot get to Europe, there are fortunes to be had."

Father loved a gamble, especially if it was certain. He was not slow to act: the results were decisive for his future – and for mine.

Meanwhile my moral compass was in a dither until, in the same place, I found a newspaper called the *Observer*, and its editorial voice, which I subsequently learnt was that of David Astor. The fact that someone else thought we were wrong, and provided fresh arguments on the subject, was a huge relief to a beleaguered schoolboy. "How could we condemn the Russians when they invaded Hungary if we behaved like this?" This was all I needed. I convinced no one at Nibley and I must have been seen as a tiresome child.

Matters moved towards resolution. Lack of US support compels Suez withdrawal, but Nibley is not surprised. "Bloody Yanks, always late for a war and now they haven't even shown up for this show." I study the speeches of John Foster Dulles and write a page in childish script about principles and politics. I compare him to Churchill, who betrayed Greece and Eastern Europe at Yalta. Sister Mo gets hold of it and reads it out at supper. There is as much hilarity at the pretension as at the spelling, but there is consternation too. Father says, "You do realise you wouldn't be alive today were it not for Winston?" and to my chagrin my mother absolutely endorses this view. My feeling of being different is strengthening.

There is Cold War resolution too on the Southern agricultural front. A back channel is opened up between the elder children on either side. A Worlock party is sent out to bring back the renegade heifers on a day when Tom Bennett is at market. There is a line of impatient traffic behind us as we come down the main road. A man in a racing-green Jaguar accelerates out of the line but cannot quite get past. He is forced back amongst the beasts, making them turn into a panicked run. As they panic so their anxious bowels evacuate Tom's good pasture grass across the front of the vehicle. Not even windscreen wipers restore vision. As we turn into Nibley Lane, I have a last view of the Jaguar on the grass verge with a furious owner raging beside it. Another bully gets his comeuppance.

A few days later an equally surreptitious work party goes out with more corrugated to repair the Iron Curtain. I do not recall that the two men ever spoke again, but their children were far more sensible.

Chapter 7

The Great Fire of Nibley

D ESPITE THE TEMPTATION to wander down Stivvies once again, searching in the banks and bends of the stream for those places where you can catch stickle-backs and imprison those tiny sea monsters in a glass jar, we must be resolute. And as we turn our backs on the field we have the full extent of the last yard, the Rickyard, before us. We stand at one end of the rectangular shape, and we can see all the way down to the other end, where the yard has its own exit onto Nibley Lane. To our immediate right are two perma-nently temporary wooden sheds, made of railway sleepers and corrugated-iron roofing. These are followed by the great range of the Dutch barn, five bays, two stories high, topped by the arched corrugated-iron roof, and as usual packed with the supplies we need for the year. The first bay has horse hay, fine May hay for the aristocrats amongst our stock. The next three are typically full of straw. Before threshing this will be in the form of ricks of sheaves, skilfully built into damp-resistant structures with heads of corn inside, the stalks pointing out. The last bay, after threshing, is often used to store the bagged corn.

We do of course have a granary. It is on the other side of the Rickyard, but you have to climb a long flight of stone steps to reach it. It is dry up there but no less rat infested than any other part of our premises. No one wants to climb stone steps with half-a-hundredweight sacks on their backs. So in the last bay we put down wooden pallets to keep the damp away. Then we stack the precious wheat, sometimes the crop from a piece of oats, and more rarely a field of barley, hoping against hope that it passes the grading and earns the highest premium price of all for barley – through sale to a brewer. The grain is covered with tarpaulins, and Father plays cat and mouse with Mr Williams, the corn merchant. Timing is everything. Mr Williams, a sombre Welshman in dark clothes, driving a huge and ancient black, hearse-like Bentley, visits frequently at times when supply and demand are under pressure. Father stresses the fact that we should not ask him to come – that would betray need – but that we should all make it clear how welcome he was when he did arrive.

The negotiations were always on a knife edge. The farmer had to get the best price for what he had – and the lowest cost on next year's seed, as well as really good quality. The seedsman was a sort of wholesaler, broking the grain to millers, animal food suppliers and brewers. His firm was based in the docks at Avonmouth, and as the two men sat gently haggling over tea or whisky in our dining room, the movement of landed grain prices or the influence of the size of the crop locally and nationally complicated the bargaining. Mr Williams produced paper and silver propelling pencil to demonstrate that a lower monetary value this year was in fact a higher price than last year, if you factored in the amount of available grain in the market.

Father would have none of it. He needed no calculations. He had a feeling, and was never wrong. Out hunting he looked over a hundred hedges. While Nibley was well placed, he saw only a bitter future in the Cotswolds. The barons of the malted-barley lands around Tetbury were taking to drink in prospect of a wheat farmer's Armageddon. He, Robert Worlock, would be smitten, yes, smitten, if his old friend Williams were reduced to kneeling on this very carpet come Michaelmas because he could not find the quality and quantity he needed.

These sessions sometimes stalled, and ended in effusive partings, regret and disappointment. More often they were in part satisfactory. Father realised some necessary cash from the Dutch barn, and got some sort of indicator of the costs for next year. The deals were done on a handshake and not recorded, or subsequently questioned, except at the year end by my mother, who managed all the farm accounts. Asked why he had sought this price or that, Father would invariably say "I had a notion", "I knew it was where he didn't want to go", or "Providence and my dear, but long dead, great-aunt were looking after me". Of these I prefer the second: Father, an instinctive gambler and a man born to bargain, almost certainly never knew what he wanted until he knew what his opponent needed.

So, you see, the Rickyard was in many ways our Treasury. Not that this was in my mind when my mother woke me up in the early hours of the morning with the words: "Get dressed quickly and come downstairs – you have to see a most terrible thing."

As I get down there Jane is pulling on her boots, and Mother shouts, "Tell your father the brigade are on their way."

We run out of the back door, and as I reach the top of the steps the whole reason for this strange interruption of the night hits me. The end section of the Dutch barn nearest Nibley Lane is alight. The dry hay in the rick here is burning fiercely. The flames are about halfway up the side of the barn, but already the heat is intense. Father is there, throwing in buckets of water from the trough, though the uselessness of this is immediately apparent.

Jane is quick and practical. "Leave that for the fire engines. We need to clear the sheds at the end."

And she is quite right. There are three young horses that Father bought at Leicester Horse Repository in the summer to sell on in the hunting season in one of the wooden tenements at the end of the barn and they are panicking. In the next shack are half a dozen steers.

"Open the field gate at the end, then let the steers out, Dave," says my sister, "while we release the horses."

I am there first and this is soon accomplished. I have to push the gate back through the horde of steers jostling to get out, but once I do they come pouring through, squeezing me between the gate and the side of the hut, and then fleeing down the hill, tails aloft, leaping and kicking. But when I turn back I see that the horses have stopped panicking. They are now standing stock still, twitching unnaturally. Father is behind them shouting and huzzahing ineffectually. Jane pulls a bridle onto another but cannot pull him forward.

"Get some sacks to cover their eyes," shouts Father.

We get three old jute bags and soak them in the water trough. With one of these on its head, the first one becomes more tractable and, once one is moving, the others, similarly garbed, become manageable as well. When they are safely released we return to the fire. One fire tender is already in place, and so are all our farm workers, as my mother is still working the phones. Half the village has turned out to see this early Bonfire Night.

But lines of volunteers passing buckets is doing no good. Once the fire hose is turned on the hay, we see the uselessness of that exercise as well. Burning hay and straw is thrown into the air. Great clouds of sparks roll upwards and out over the other yards, the house, the village … There are now three tenders in place and the fire chief tells us that the best they can do is to direct the hoses onto the underside of the roof, so the water falls from there onto the flames:

"But we cannot save the barn or its contents, we can just supervise the burnout."

Can we yet save some of the bags of wheat and barley in the fifth bay, the one furthest from the flames? We rush down to try. Someone backs up a tractor and trailer but the tangle of machines and hoses frustrates us. And while the flames now consume the first bay, the second bay, which has baled straw, seems untouched. What we in the front do not know is that the fire has spread rapidly along the back of the barn. When we go to pull away sacks of wheat they are already hot. Someone pulls a sack forward and flames shoot out behind it. The firemen usher us away.

And at this point I must leave the scene. We are running short of water. I am told to help move the milking herd out of Sixteen Acres, the field across the road from Stivvies, and then direct the fire tenders to refill with water from the old quarry in the wood beyond it. By the time I return, the sky is beginning to lighten and the fullest fury of the fire is over. The three tenders are still spraying water up into the roof and, indeed, will still be doing that at noon. Villagers have departed. Horses and steers have been recaptured and penned. Ben is getting the milking shed ready for morning milking, but I cannot take my eyes off the shaking, inconsolable figure sitting hunched on the granary steps.

Somewhere in the last few hours Father has moved beyond the disaster of fire and into the cataclysm of ruin. We shall be bankrupt. Penniless and homeless. It has befallen his family before and now here it was again visiting the next generation. Much more was incomprehensible, and I felt relieved when the fire chief came over.

"You and your sister should take him indoors now. There is nothing more he can do here. Thank your mother for all the tea and coffee through the long night."

We walked him up the yard, one on either side, tears running down his face. Installed at the kitchen table, I began to eat hungrily. My mother sat beside Father and began gently to ease him back down.

"Well, at least the insurance is good – Arthur made sure we went comprehensive." (Her eldest brother was manager of Eagle Star Insurance in Gloucester.) And then, moments later, "Nice Major Ashby who was Don's best friend in the Indian Army is now our manager at the Midland – he has already offered us a bigger overdraft." And then "No horses, or people for that matter, were killed or injured…"

Soon he too was strengthening his resolve with sausage, bacon and eggs, and, since workers and well wishers kept coming in, the kitchen was soon a lively place of anecdote and reminiscing about the night's events. It was at this point that two sleepy figures in pyjamas appeared around the kitchen door.

"What is happening down here? Why all the noise?"

My sisters, Mo and Mary, snug in the front bedroom, had slept through the Great Fire of Nibley.

Despite the good insurance policy, we were soon awash with loss adjusters and claims evaluators. We were all interviewed: one of them accused me of being a secret smoker who had gone out for a crafty drag. My mother and chaperone was scandalised and the question was withdrawn.

Every farm worker had a theory about vengeance arson: "It were that bloke the boss cussed out the other day, he said he'd be back."

From disappointed tradesmen, to rejected trainee farmhands, to gypsies thrown off the premises, the list grew and grew. Yet we all knew that spontaneous combustion in the fierce warmth generated in a hayrick had often caused such events to occur.

Finally, the police solved a crime they were not even investigating. A man arrested for something else confessed to getting drunk at the Swan, being unable to cycle home, climbing into the hay for some sleep, lighting up for a last drag before dozing off, then scaring himself with the flames and cycling off in a hurry…

Chapter 8

Father: A Man on Horseback

ASK YOURSELF WHEN and in what situations you feel most natural and in touch with life. The answer can be interesting. Had you asked Father then the answer would have been clear and unequivocal. On the back of a horse. And from my formative years I began to accumulate reasons for this. Horseback gave authority. You could bark orders from up there with less fear of contradiction than if you were on the ground. You could carry weapons of war – in this case a long stock whip with a horn handle and a vicious crack – which looked slightly over the top at ground level. And when herding stock you did not have to run about so much as we children did.

As I got older and more observant I also saw that horseback was a refuge from other people's authority. A man on a nervous wheeling animal, or even on an animal being made to wheel restlessly, is far less susceptible to instructions issued at ground level, whether by his mother in his earlier years or my mother in my early years. In fact, once mounted I believe he felt released, and given that he rode, exercising or hunting, every day of his life from early youth into his early eighties, then we are looking at someone who felt the pressure of many fetters of duty and responsibility. And you may even find traces of guilt and shame over unjust accusations of a failure to perform, accusations which he perhaps inherited and passed on a generation. Here we are on dangerous ground and you must make up your own minds.

If you are to do that, then I must quickly sketch in the rest of the equine picture. So what did the man look like on horseback?

"Like a sack of potatoes," said his great friend, and fellow hunter, Jack Windell, who farmed the prestigious Home Farm on the Badminton Estate.

During the long and fruitless years when I was being taught to ride, the urgings of my sisters and the barked orders of Father ingrained in me an idea of how you sat on a horse.

He would shout, "Straight back, lean forward, knees gripping, heels in, hands two inches above the pummel," until my fear of getting it wrong, and a natural lack of co-ordination that to this day sets me checking my left hand from my right, forced me into curse-inducing error once again.

But though he knew how he wanted me to ride, and although Mo and Mary rode that way, Father did not. He had a tendency to slouch backwards in the saddle, back far from straight. As a result his feet often stretched forward, and when he was tired his hands could fall, and he found that the saddle was an easy place for light sleep. A natural rider with an instinctive understanding of his mount, he was in full and absolute control when he needed to be, but was lucky his horses knew their own way home when he did not. Some of this style deficit he blamed on learning to ride without a saddle. He used to ride his pony, Billy, to school in Tetbury as a ten-year-old, and I later remember him telling me of the first dance he ever attended, in the room above the bar at the Kingscote Arms. A shy teenager, he came up the hill from Tresham, where his grandparents lived, on his horse and left it in the pub stables.

"And did you dance with the girls?" was my first question.

"No, not at all," he said, a vestige of the shyness and embarrassment of that evening still in his face. "You see, I had no saddle. I was fearful of being late so I pushed the pony on a bit coming up the hill. He sweated up a bit, and the back of my legs and backside got so coated with sweat and horsehair that I sat with my back to the wall until we all went home."

Here we are faced with another conundrum. One clear facet of Father is "the man who loved horses". He probably spent the major part of his conscious life talking about, thinking about, cleaning or sitting astride a horse. As we shall see, he loved the business of buying a horse. Weighing up the tasks. History of lameness in the right foreleg? Cannon-bones been fired? Broken by an Irish dealer with a twitch on the nose? Teeth don't match the owner's claims about the age of the animal? Here was a real enjoyment – matching risk to price to discern value. Here you could see the dealer's adrenaline running in Father, but did it really add up to a love for a horse, as distinct from horses at large?

It is easy to conjure up a picture of him as a lonely child, with a prematurely dead father, and a preoccupied mother. The ten-year-old eldest boy, with no companionship of his own age, always in the company of Billy the pony, fixated and deeply in love with the horse in all its forms. As in any speculation I am sure there is some buried truth here. But not the whole truth. For one marked characteristic of Father in his life with horses was a total lack of sentimentality. Did this horse lover let horses who had served him well for many years live out their lives in a sunlit paddock? Did this lover of horses believe that he could make riders of his children by buying suitable ponies? (Only once in these years, when he bought Robin, a beautiful chestnut Arab pony for Mary, did he break the otherwise inflexible rule that children should ride horses.)

While an old cob called Twist was kept for domestic purposes, which ranged from stock management to pulling a horse hoe, everything else was in a constant state of flux. A visit to Leicester produced the perfect hunt horse. Lord X or the Hon Mrs Y wanted a bay gelding just like that and perfection was quickly despatched in their direction if the price was right. The great bargain that was found unsound in wind and limb when brought home rapidly went for glue. The sound and trustworthy jumper that lasted two seasons rarely did three. Was it boredom? Or the instinctive drives of the dealer? And was the absence of sentimental attachment a derivative of the unhappy decade of his teenage years, or the natural response of the farmer to all animals as goods and chattels?

Father also loved dogs, but in the same unsentimental way. He often spoke of an old dog from his youth, of their mutual regard and hours spent together, and of her skill with sheep and young cattle (far greater than mine, clearly). But one day he saw she was going blind so he picked up a spade, took her down to the wood, hit her on the back of the head and killed and buried her. I have no way of knowing if this was true, but I believed him instantly. He did not seem to get attached in the way I did.

In old age he mellowed a bit, but I still wonder if the emotionally detached "man who didn't care" was a conscious act to protect himself from sadness or disappointment, or whether it was a real patina formed by these emotions in his teenage years, as real as the scabs and scars on his horny old hands. Those hands which could be put under nearly boiling water without apparent feeling. Those hands from which the very flesh was always being picked or peeled or bitten. How much feeling he really experienced – on his hands or in his emotions – remains an issue in the search for the man who was Father.

Chapter 9

A Day in Wednesday Country

Now that we have our man on horseback, it is time that we dealt with the proper business of riding. Hunting. Please first note the language. We have not spoken of horse riding or of fox hunting. Father was insistent on the proper use of language. As he explained, if you spoke of "riding", a horse was assumed amongst educated, civilised people. Likewise "hunting" could only in England involve a fox. And you never referred to people hunting in red coats, or riding white horses. Hunting pink, please, and grey. Otherwise you were called an abominable heretic and held up to ridicule. For the first thing we have to understand about hunting foxes is that we are not talking about a sport, though we shall find some sporting aspects later on. In this year, in 1955, I began to discover that hunting was a language, a religion, a form of exclusive club with non-exclusive followers, a way of expressing rejection of urban life (and sometimes of the twentieth century). What it was certainly not was a group of like-minded folk dedicated to killing foxes and shouting "tally ho!" Indeed foxes came to seem almost an accidental appendage to the whole business.

And religions need to have high priests. Around my tenth year I made a connection that afterwards seemed so obvious that I had to hope no one had noticed that I had not latched on earlier. Father's conversation was peppered with references to "His Grace". Now I knew this did not refer to a clergyman – regular objects of ridicule – but the individual was obviously held in the highest reverence. I also knew that the most power-ful man in our area was the Duke of Beaufort. I knew that in previous generations we had been tenants of the great land-owner, whose 58,000 acre estate, centred on Badminton House, was sometimes known as Beaufortshire. I had been there, every year, for the Three Day Event, the great equestrian festival which the current duke had founded, and where I had seen my father, as a steward, riding between fences on cross-country day, blowing his whistle and using the same sort of language on hapless pedestrians who did not clear a way for the riders quickly enough as he used on us children and the innocent heifers in the Yate road.

So on that rare day, when I was ten and the Beaufort Hunt actually drew the woods at Westerleigh, I was unready for revelations. A fox was hunted as far as our small coppice at the bottom of Sixteen Acres. Seeing the direction of travel, Father came racing down the Nibley Lane as if he was bringing the news from Aix to Ghent, and shouted at me:

"Stand by the Sixteen Acres gate until His Grace comes by, then open up and let him through."

At last I was to meet His Grace, and I did not have long to wait. First came a few stray hounds, then a perspiring kennel huntsman, in the green jacket denoting those hunt servants involved in hunting hounds. He was riding point (that is, he was an observant outrider), then a whipper-in with the main body of hounds, and, after these altar boys and archimandrites, came the Duke of Beaufort, Master of Foxhounds, a middle-aged man with steel-rimmed spectacles and a "never surprised" expression.

The whipper-in said, "We lost him across the railway line, Your Grace," and my shock was so complete that for a moment I forgot to open the gate. The Duke and His Grace were one and the same person. We used "Your Grace" to designate him as a living god. It was all a bit reminiscent of the Holy Trinity. Your Grace, the Master, the Duke. Suddenly, for some reason, I felt a lot clearer about matters theological and cosmological.

And I did open the gate. As I did the great man leant down in the saddle and said,

"Are you Robert Worlock's son?"

When I stuttered out an affirmative, the great man nodded as if he knew that to be the case, continued to look unsurprised, and proceeded wordlessly into the field. These were the only words I ever exchanged with Henry Somerset, 10th Duke of Beaufort, and I treasure them. He was followed by the Spanish Inquisition in the form of Major Gerald Gundry, Field Master, who snapped at me,

"Is there a gate on the other side of this field? Can His Grace get out?"

But then rode off at a canter, leaving his questions hanging in the air. Other prelates and cardinals followed: some in hunt colours of blue and buff (a strange reminder of the Whig aristocracy from which Tory Badminton emerged), some in pink (the garb of visitors and guests), many wearing toppers. These were the true gentry, or rich enough to dress like them. Their horses were immaculate and the aroma of neat's-foot oil, saddle soap, sweat and Jermyn St cologne soon filled the air in equal parts. And while most of the women in this group rode astride, I still recall the precarious passage (how much more courageous they were than their male counterparts) of three ladies, veiled and hair in snoods, riding side-saddle.

Behind all of this dignity come the hunting farmers. This group is mostly in black hunting jackets, wearing bowlers or black hunting caps. Hard hats are mandatory for all. The jackets are long, covering the thighs of the rider in the saddle, made of thick thorn-proof material and having huge, deep pockets. Father's pockets at this time contain a hip flask of port and one of brandy, and my mother has, as we have seen, included a generous slice of sustaining fruit cake. Which reminds me, as the yeoman farmers are followed by sundry other ranks, children and camp followers in rat-catcher jackets, where is Father in this orderly parade?

This group of what could be up to two hundred riders is called the "field", and on this day it moves along with exemplary order under the command of Major Gundry. The major sees the value of discipline. His job is to see that order is preserved to the point where two hundred horses do not trample growing crops, fences are not smashed down by attempts to jump them, that mounted followers keep to lanes and tracks where possible and that two horsemen (well, often women, or mostly girls) are delegated to bring up the rear and close all the gates after everyone has passed through.

But Father is not with these, nor is he gossiping with the fellowship of girl grooms out in the lane, riding the "second horses" which the very wealthy will call for after lunch when their initial mount has tired. He is nowhere to be seen. Does this mean that he is not a true courtier of His Grace? Not at all. When you get close to him you will see that his black jacket is buttoned with black buttons, each bearing the initials "B.H." picked out in gold lettering. His Grace has awarded Father the Hunt Button, the first XI colours, reserved for those most loyal followers and subscribers who form the Praetorian Guard. As the field form up on the left to observe the work of the hunt and see the Duke "drawing" the covert by bringing hounds through it to catch a scent and then force a fox to break cover and make a dash for it, his absence seems almost disloyal.

To understand him at all we need to understand why, at this moment, he is now a quarter mile away, on the other side of the little wood, on his own behind a clump of trees, listening to the Duke's horn which tells him exactly where hounds are and what they are doing. He is in a state of high excitement. Throughout the covert drawing ceremony he is holding horse and rider as motionless as possible. Until, that is, he sees what he expects to see, and hears "gone away" on the horn to confirm it.

Father is a hunting fanatic and a lifelong loyalist of the Duke. It is just that his religious observances are not as others. Not for him the good order of the field. In a hunting life that is to last seventy years, his study of foxes and countryside and the way things generally turn out has led him to make a series of bets with himself. He actually feels that he knows where the fox will run and though he knows there will be another horseman nearby (a junior kennel huntsman with a whistle posted to signal if fox and hounds come out that way) he knows that if he gets it right then he can enjoy some moments of pure joy. From this we learn three other very strong characteristics of

Father: his disregard for order and love of rule breaking; his pronounced gambling streak, not exercised on a racecourse but in predicting outcomes and beating the odds; and his driving hedonism, identifying what gave him pleasure and pursuing it single-mindedly all of his life.

Which brings us to the point of the pleasure itself. Those who are not convinced that pleasure is an isolated high will point to the contributory elements surrounding Father's moments of ecstasy. He described these moments in terms of feeling "most alive", of "what makes it worth going on", and in late middle-age he frequently said that "If I knew I couldn't feel like that again I would rather end it all then and there."

Something vitally important, a compound built up from his sense of occasion, his reverence for the hunting tradition, his love of the horse and his skilled horsemanship, his knowledge of the country and estimation of the likely performance of hunter and hunted – all these contributed to the build up to these moments. But then something else took over at that moment when the whistle sounded or fox or hounds broke cover. We can speak easily of an adrenaline rush, of a "red haze", and of masters of several packs who urged him to keep himself under control. That was always going to be too much to ask. At this point, if luck held, he knew the supreme excitement of embarking upon the chase itself.

So let us follow him, just behind hounds (but often uncomfortably ahead of master and huntsmen). We cross a piece of pasture with a wall on the far side. Father unerringly chooses a place where he is on rising ground, which minimises the height of the obstacle but faces horse and rider with a steep drop on the other side. Hounds have checked, and now turn at right angles to the previous direction – the glory of not knowing what happens next – and race across a field of kale.

Father pounds up one edge and, at the top, finds a hedge with a very jumpable rail re-enforcing it, giving access to a grass ley, well established, which he feels he can cross to catch hounds as they check at the stream. The Master hurries down to the gate and the little bridge, but Father puts his horse at the post-and-rails in front of the water. And this is what he describes as "the moment". Would he clear the fence? Was his jump big enough to get him onto the bank at the far side? How steep was that bank? Was there a barbed-wire or electric fence on the far side to keep livestock out? Freeze-frame Father in the air above the stream and amidst that complexity of risk. This is what he has come for and this is glorious happiness and he will seek it twice a week for a lifetime.

In the next field the fox has disobligingly gone to ground in an ozier bed. The Master warns Father, yet again, of the dangers of riding too close to hounds and when, after ten minutes, the field does finally arrive, requests that the field master instruct Mr Worlock to stay with the field. But, certainly by his later years with the Heythrop, he knows it is all in vain. Father is not effectively in control, of others or of himself. He has forgotten that he brought two of his children with him this morning. Hopefully they are still with the field. He is unimpressed by the lady who warns him that he might have been badly hurt at the stream: he has fallen many times, stoically suffered many broken bones, but always returns to the pleasure point. Without risk these days would be nothing.

Perhaps it is wise to step back now. Hunting is a banned activity and an unfashionable topic. But one thing is clear: however we examine the pleasures of hunting, they were central to Father's life. He not only sought them continuously over a seventy-year period, but he financed them over that time too, through good times and bad.

It is hard to recall a time when each season did not see new mounts at Nibley and latterly at Heath End. Some of these costs were offset by selling and dealing in horses, but hunting was still an expensive business. Fortunately, when Beaufort subscriptions started at around £1000, hunting farmers who made their land available were only capped at £100. But considering that Father sent three of his four children to boarding schools, maintained a high standard of living and, though family holidays were a rarity, appeared to lack for little, many observers, and not least his brothers-in-law, wondered how hunting could be afforded.

The answer is simple: it came first, and after it everything else had to be afforded. And there is little doubt that this was a foundational agreement of his marriage as well. Allow those two, or sometimes three, days a week of winter pleasure, and all that went to make it possible throughout the year, and he would do everything else required of him. And that bargain was kept, the fruit cake always in the pocket, the hip flasks filled, the excuses loyally made to children, friends and relatives until we all understood. Hunting comes first.

Chapter 10

Hunting: Falls and Fractures

LET FATHER SUM UP his hunting career in his own words. On his eightieth birthday the Heythrop Hunt held a celebratory meet on the lawn of Heath End Farm to which my parents and I, sole child left at home and just about to go to Cambridge, had moved in 1963. But now we are in 1988, and *Horse and Hound* have sent a photographer who records a rare picture of Father in hunting clothes standing beside his two brothers, John and Dick. We shall meet these two again later. But for now we should look at the paragraph which Father dictates to the rather shocked young man, and later confirmed on the telephone when they wanted to verify the spellings. Here is the piece:

On Wednesday 21st December the Heythrop Hounds met at Heath End Farm, Evenlode, Moreton-in-Marsh to celebrate Mr. Robert Worlock's 80th birthday. Hospitality was extended to a field of nearly two hundred and many foot-followers. Mr Richard Sumner, Heythrop Joint Master, made a short speech in honour of the host before hounds moved off. Robert Worlock's seventy years of riding to hounds started as a boy with his father following Mr Herbert Nell's hounds in the Sodbury Vale. He hunted with the Berkeley and the Beaufort between the wars and moved to Heath End Farm 25 years ago. He enjoyed 13 seasons with Capt. Wallace and also hunted with the late Duke of Beaufort and Mr Hastings Neal. He continues to ride with the Heythrop every Wednesday and Saturday, and does his own horse at the end of the day. He has walked puppies for both the Heythrop and Beaufort and his latest cup winner was Rosary at Peterborough in 1986.

Like all vanity publishing this needs a bit of decoding. For example, the confining of reference to his hunting with the Beaufort to the interwar years, when they extended almost twenty years after, shows a man who has changed his loyalties and follows fresh gods. The reference to Herbert Nell reminds us that Father's own father died in 1918, when Father was ten. Herbert Nell, wealthy local landowner, became a father figure and an advisor on valuing and buying horses for many years. His presence here covers the years before Father becomes wholly under the spell of His Grace. Hastings Neal, celebrated M.F.H. and, as a hunting writer second only to G. Whyte-Melville in Father's estimation, appears here to show that the octogenarian is a man of wide reading and experience, not just the reflection of the two masters he has followed all his life. The reference to doing his own horses is intended to excite our sympathy for an old man whose daughters, who long ago did this for him, do so no more, and he cannot afford a girl groom. None of his family members who walked all of those puppies will be at all surprised at his claiming the prize!

How do we square the changing loyalties noted above? Time and guilt would seem the probable answers. As soon as he was financially able to do so Father left Nibley, increasingly urbanising into Yate–Sodbury, for the glorious North Cotswold countryside in which he was to spend the rest of his life. My mother became, for the first time in her life, a presence in a village community and an active member of the Red Cross and other village fund-raising societies, including the village fête. But these are incremental advantages alongside the main drive behind Father's decision. And it is Father's decision. He attends the sale of Heath End Farm with his bank manager, having agreed to buy it if he can, but having set a bidding limit agreed by both spouse and banker. Once that limit is reached it is he who goes on bidding, he who breaks the rule and gets the prize, and they who must accept what has been accomplished.

He just had to have it. Though a small acreage and not particularly productive as a farm, it was right in the centre of prime Heythrop Hunt country. Just as the Heythrop had broken with the Beaufort in the nineteenth century to form a separate hunt in north Gloucestershire so Father was about to break with the 10th Duke. Hunting had deteriorated at Badminton. In old age His Grace seemed less able to provide sport. Yet a younger man, Captain Ronnie Wallace, had taken on the mastership of the Heythrop, and was spoken of as the heir apparent, both as a huntsman and a hound judge. Many were going north to a hunt that always "found" a fox and had a growing record of good runs. Father mused on how many seasons he might have left. He worried about his family's ancient loyalty to the Duke; would His Grace see this as desertion? Despite intermediaries who attempted to explain why Robert Worlock was going, I know that Father always felt that the Duke thought less of him. Whether that was true or not I have no way of knowing.

After Father had been hunting with Capt Wallace for about five years and had established a reputation for derring-do and rank indiscipline, the master sought to honour him, and perhaps make him a little more tractable. He offered him the Heythrop Button. Looking down at his hunting jacket, still complete with Beaufort Button, he is said to have replied,

"I thank you, master, it is a great honour. But you see these buttons have been on my coat a long time, and do a good job of keeping my jacket closed, so I must decline."

Since I was told this story by several others I am inclined to believe it is substantially true. Certainly the offer was never repeated, and we have a right to wonder if the story was meant to get back to the ageing Duke. Memories of the kindness of that grandee to his mother and his brother John, a Badminton Estate tenant, would have been there. Above all, Father wanted to retain the respect of the Master, the man who to him embodied Hunting.

Did other things worry him about making the move some sixty miles north? I see no evidence that leaving two of his daughters and his grandchildren behind caused misgivings, nor apparently did leaving his aged in-laws, then living with increasing difficulty in a large house in the Bristol suburbs and dependent on their daughter, our mother, for support and organisation. He may even have felt a little relieved, not much missing his father-in-law's weekly visits. In time the care of the elderly maternal grandparents fell to these two sisters of mine, Jane and Mary, and when the journey south proved too much for my own parents, these two journeyed north to offer their support as their parents aged. Father would have been the first to admit that families survive through such selflessness, but he just knew he had to get to Wallace and enjoy hunting's last hurrah!

Not that even the hunting itself was without its problems and pitfalls. Horses were unreliable. Animals were apt to deteriorate in wind and limb (we once had a gelding with a tube and a stopper in his throat, the Hobday operation, and it taxed Father's powers of concentration to recall when the stopper should be in or out). Horses sworn to be sound by fellow hunting men sometimes proved to be lame: the lamentations over this deceit prompted nothing self-reflective in Father, who never recalled his own omissions and exaggerations when he was the seller, and then there were the facts of a hard working life.

Father was 55 when he came into the magnetic orbit of Ronnie Wallace. That magnetism did not end with the four heiress wives who had supported Wallace's hunting life. There was some left for the farmers who had to be kept on side to allow hunting to continue, and their wives and families all got sucked into the legend of the master who always found. Naysayers who claimed to have seen foxes trapped in the wilds of Acocks Green or Solihull, "sprung" from a hessian bag when the first draw of a covert proved unproductive, were dismissed by Father as "damned heretics". Yet even he wondered, in the year when Yells Oziers flooded completely, and we feared we had no fox to offer up since none had been seen there all season. We need not have worried. The master still found.

And the thrills and spills of the subsequent chase! These, he said, were his greatest hunting days. There were certainly spills. Not just the nearly moments so breathlessly recounted by my sister Mo in wonderful narratives that always began, "I nearly fell off." Father did fall off, quite and increasingly often, and he was lucky on a number of occasions not to have ended his hunting life in the process. Each instance became an anecdote which grew into a legend. Since I cannot testify to the height of the fences, the breadth of the rivers, or the speed of the chase, I can only give you a view of how one of these events was experienced from the outside.

It is an early January morning, at the beginning of the 1970s, and I am down for the weekend. I had only recently officially learnt to drive on roads, and though I had great familiarity with the Land Rover I had no experience of it with a horse trailer – and a horse – on behind. This did not interest Father. He loaded up, got into the passenger seat and said, "The Meet is at Great Tew, so that is the last place we are going to go to."

So we set off. I had realised that Father did not go to Meets some time before. He hated the social side. As a man with no small talk except hunting, why would he? But when I asked him where he did want to go, he simply said, "The Right Place," so we proceeded in silence until I was ordered to drive off the lane and up a farm track to an isolated barn with a yard in front of it. There we stopped, unloaded the horse and detached the horse box. When I asked if the farmer would mind us leaving it there I just got a pitying look. Mounted, Father then headed off through a gate, replying to my enquiry,

"Wallace will draw Falklands or Dennison's Copse first, and I need to be in the right place. Follow on in the Land Rover and try to keep up. And shut this gate behind me."

By the time I reached the village the Meet was over, and I followed the long line of car followers to a vantage point on a grass verge, where wizened countrymen gazed at distant woodland through mist and binoculars, while offering a cupped ear and a hoarse "'ear that?" in encouragement. After a moment I did see the huntsman on point at the edge of the covert and I did hear "Gone Away" on the horn. The latter was like a signal. The ancients flew back to their vehicles in Le Mans Start style and we all raced up the road until we reached the next Grass Verge of Silent Contemplation. Here we resumed our religious duties until the silence was broken by a stout lady with two terriers on leads. She was shouting.

"Mr Worlock"s son?" I climbed over the gate and met her half way. "Your father fell at the rails," she said. "Horse pecked on landing and he went over the side. Pity was he left his foot in the stirrup. Horse dragged him to the top of the field where the whipper-in caught it by the gate. We've sent a second horse to ring for an ambulance and there was a doctor out today who's with him now."

There was indeed a man in pink kneeling beside him when I got there. He lay under a hawthorn bush and seemed dreadfully still to me.

The man stood up and said, "He is conscious but needs some pain relief – I can't begin to imagine what he has done to his foot and ankle. Keep him still until the ambulance comes."

He then remounted and resumed his sport, and I become aware of a young man holding Father's horse.

"We caught 'un!" he says, and in a tone that clearly signifies that he deserves a reward.

Then the gate closers arrive and peer down from their horses.

"Hope the ambulance gets here soon," says one, a very capable-sounding middle-aged lady. "Look, there is a groom taking a lame horse home in the road – let her take Robert's horse as well and then we can let your mother know where you can collect it from."

Suddenly the field is empty. Everyone is so kind, but Father seems now very small, his hands very cold. They had put his riding hat beside his head and I move it to one side to stroke his fine hair, still hardly grey, and begin to wonder about whether this was the last great fall when I hear the ambulance siren. Soon two strong men are loading him onto a stretcher.

"John Radcliffe Hospital!" they shout as they climb aboard.

I run back to the Land Rover, with a deepening conviction that he will not survive the journey. How will I explain that I was the last person to see him alive? Would he want to be buried in full hunting regalia, just as he lay in that field, including his latest and proudest acquisition, his historic hunting boots, said to have been made in 1876 for his great-great-grandfather? I come up behind the ambulance on the main road and stay five feet behind it all the way down the Woodstock Road and into the yard of the old Radcliffe.

Two porters hurry to the back door of the ambulance. I am so sure I am right but so hope I am wrong that I abandon the Land Rover in front of the entrance, engine running, door open, and dash to join them.

As the corpse descends to the gurney, it intones, "Yes, I know my leg is swollen, dammit. Not a complete idiot! But it will go down in time. In the meanwhile let no snivelling idiot of a matron try to cut my boots off. Damn and blast you, these boots must be preserved at all costs."

Relieved that he was still alive and still Father, I went back to park the vehicle.

By a miracle they did save the boots, but in a surgeon's revenge his broken foot was wired, and he lost the use of the joints in his toes. This meant that his straight toes would not fit his historic boots – until, that is, he had the necessary metatarsal amputation performed. It was the least he could do for hunting.

Chapter 11

Unreliable Witnesses

L ET'S LEAVE Father for a moment, expostulating wildly to the largely unimpressed nurses in the John Radcliffe. This secure and confident figure, acting out his role of yeoman farmer safe in his own acres, is a very different person from the farmer we met earlier in 1955, and a very different individual from the boy who watched his father die in 1918. Three people can fill in that background: my grandfather, my grandmother and Father himself. But we must be careful, for each of these will have an axe to grind, and although the latter pair were prolific tellers of family stories, they saw no particular virtue in being consistent in the telling, and both specialised in adjusting the tale to the listener. But we are in pursuit of his *story*, not history. We are not here to iron out versioning, but just to tell a story.

Let's start with the most unknowable. Who was Robert Thomas Worlock, Father's father, and how did his ideas and upbringing influence his son? Interestingly, Father's own picture of the Worlocks was that they were strugglers – "climbing, generation after generation, up the crack in the hills from Wotton (Wotton-under-Edge: 'Wotton Undridge' locally) and Dursley until they got to the top of the Kilcott valley and could enjoy the rich farming of the Cotswold top lands."

This sense of a generational voyage, of a mission to leave the small muddy fields of the Severn Vale for the rich and expansive barley country on the Cotswold escarpment is powerful family mythology. My great-grandfather had made it to the small village of Tresham, just off the top of the hill. Here, as he got older, he had increasingly handed the reins to the son. Father had happy memories of his grandparents, and particularly of the women of the house. His grandmother and great-aunt were regularly cited, along with blessed Providence, as the forces whose prayers and heavenly intercessions kept him safe. No mention here of God in this cosmology: those with a keen ear, though out of the hearing of my mother, averred that he was not a strong believer in anything.

Father always spoke of his father and his grandfather as "good farmers", strongly motivated to get as much out of the soil as they could while putting in as little as possible. Indeed they had little choice, in the age before the ability to restore soil fertility with chemical nitrogen. They knew, however, that legumes fixed nitrogen back in the soil, so the rotation of corn crops with beans or rape or roots improved the quality and quantity of subsequent corn production. Manure from livestock helped too, at the cost of increasing weeds as well. Lime could be applied, but since everything had to be moved and spread by men with horses, the number of interventions one could afford was limited. Judging by the Betjeman-patent tantalus on our sideboard, inscribed as an award to Robert Thomas Worlock in 1885 by the Chippenham Agricultural Association for "the best crop of roots", father and son were recognised as good practitioners by their peers. But war, so often kind to farmers, proved a disaster to my grandfather when it came in 1914. Father takes up the story in a letter of 7 June 1987, in the context of a conversation about "stress".

Worry was the old expression of it, and I will never forget its dreadful visitation upon my poor father in World War 1. It destroyed all his good rotational farming and, having taken away arbitrarily three young men and four young horses, home bred all, the instruction was 'plough more land'.

The Western Front had to be fed with more young men and confiscated horses. The farmers had to produce more food to sustain a wartime population. The gradually improving agricultural prosperity after the Great Depression of the 1870s had enabled these Worlocks to climb up the valley to modest prosperity in Tresham before the war. Then it was gone, but before that disaster, Robert Thomas married Ethel Marguerite Hatherall and settled down to family life. They were to have four children. William Robert George, the subject of this book, was the eldest. He was followed by John, then Queenie, who died of consumption in her twenties. Lastly came Richard Thomas, always known as Dick, and to my grandmother as "the Peach", her clear and unambiguous favourite. We shall talk about the relationships between these children elsewhere, but that story begins in 1908 with Father's birth.

The anecdotes of my grandmother painted her and her young husband as a dashing couple. She and her brothers were from a slightly wealthier background with a stronger social identity. She described her courtship in romantic terms, pointing out this clump of trees as the one where he waited on horseback for her return from Tetbury, or that barn as the scene of a dance or a party.

You were left with the impression of a strong-willed young woman, the life and soul of the party. In her own expression she was a "go-er", and she identified and defended my sister Mo, at a time when she was facing parental criticism for her social life, as a fellow go-er. For Gran, being a go-er meant getting everything you could out of life. It meant hedonism with a slightly more relaxed moral code than was conventional at that time. With good social connections (her mother was a Garlick, from nearby Beverston Castle) a varied social life could be maintained. And you needed a little money (in extremes, access to a skilled abortionist would be risky and expensive if required).

The stories of romantic courtship perhaps covered a sense that she had married beneath her station by half a notch. Her sister Kath married the prosperous and very stylish local auctioneer, Critchley Pope. But when the young couple married, Robert Thomas at least made a social catch, and in 1908 their firstborn son arrived. In a village with plenty of childcare, in the form especially of a doting mother-in-law and a maiden aunt, she was never going to be prime carer and after the wet nurse had departed Father was mostly in the hands of the previous generation. As Gran said, children were boring before they could talk, and insolent afterwards. On a visit to relatives with her, my cousin Robert and I had the temerity to ask why people had children.

"Why, to carry on the family farming and look after their parents when they get old," was the immediate response. A statement of the obvious in her terms.

One day, in my teenage years, after working scything nettles and clipping grass around the graves in Tresham churchyard, Father and I strolled in the evening light down through the village and stopped outside a cottage where a man was bent digging in his front garden. Greetings were exchanged, I was introduced to the digger, and enquiries made between the men as to health and happiness. As we strolled away, it occurred to me to remark on how much alike the two men had looked, which made Father smile. He told me that this man had been the village postman, and also Father's childhood companion, since they were close in age. He then told me about the relationship that they shared, and I am afraid that I tucked it into the back of my head as a bit of a yarn until I re-read his letter to me of 23 February 1992:

Hounds meeting at Tresham last week was the opportunity for Dick to take Joyce and others around the churchyard. And all the weight of stone that sat on once short lives. How lustily my father sang the well known hymns here only to resign it all at 39 after 2 days in bed. I remember how John Miller Rev.d had to speak firmly to him for his craving for a fairly frequent drinking session in doubtful company at Wotton – 'twas his only little vice that I ever heard of except that case of the girl's fertility which may have been expensive. The boy was a great pal of mine when young and our resemblance was sometimes remarked upon casually.

And this reference was clearly on his mind, since he had first raised it the previous year when talking about the social class and the aspirations of the Worlocks:

However, I was persuaded that there was a certain nobility of *mien* in our 'name' at Tresham, which commanded 'respect', which also being translated meant 'keep yourself up' (a very favourite saying of his mother). When father strayed into forbidden bedrooms achieving unwanted posterity it did little to help! But Joe Clark's son, at about this same time, fell flat (?) because of the desecration (sic) of Elias (Elaine?) Watts, that was quite different. He explained before the JP (Justice of the Peace) that it could not be the case (that she was pregnant by him).

But 'twas proved. And Dan had to pay! 'Twas not so much the paying that hurt so much as the father's pride. The cause of Christ failed against that of Beelzebub. Oh for a bit of rubber! All past history is besmirched by the failings of one man.

And what do we make of these stories? Apart from the cost of paying off the servant girl, Father does not seem at all morally perplexed by his own father's extra-marital affairs or his frequenting the bordellos of Wotton. Uncle Dick, not a good witness since he was an infant when his father died, spoke wryly of the time taken of an evening "penning up the chickens against foxes", seemingly a family expression for what kept my grandfather from his hearth. We may ask also whether a great deal of moral opprobrium fell on Grandfather as a result of these acts. While the clergyman knew and the village knew, as long as mother and child were looked after in that rather closed community other forms of censure or ostracism were avoided. My grandmother projected her late husband as a romantic hero and a loving man who liked a drink and was not wiser as a result. We do not need to be social historians to know that late-Victorian social attitudes were very differently expressed by the urban middle classes than they were in isolated Cotswold villages.

The anecdote also raises interesting questions about my grandmother and her own struggle. There was bound to have been stress, and keeping up appearances, and Hatherall relatives insinuating that she had married beneath herself. Then he was dead. She could not go on living with her in-laws. So she moved back to her beloved Calcot Manor, where she had given birth to Father (in a servant's room above the great kitchen – now a comfortable bedroom in a very successful country-house hotel).

She threw in her lot with her delinquent brothers, and by her account did more farming than either of them. She certainly became a proficient cattle dealer with a reputation for striking a hard bargain.

These years must have been indescribably tough, a widow with four children, deeply dependent on parents and in-laws until the Great Crash of 1929 followed by the consequent agricultural depression. Better farmers than the Hatheralls were ruined. Their neighbours and relatives at nearby Beverston Castle, the Garlicks, beloved of Father for their kindness to him in his youth, lost their home farm. It is small wonder that this whole generation, my Gran and Father most strongly, were marked by fear of financial failure, and the necessity to have male children to come forward and join the labour force and ensure survival for dependents young and old.

But young Robert, Father in this narrative, was ten, not ready to join anyone's labour force. And he had to go to school, so he rode Billy the pony into Tetbury to the Dame school there every morning. His mother, while not very sympathetic to children, did realise that he had to learn farming and have some male role models in his life So he was sent nearby to the villages of Culkerton and Leighterton. The two prosperous farmers who dominated these villages, as the Worlocks had Tresham, were Dan and Stan Clark, related to my grandmother but of a totally different cast of mind to her. These shrewd and clever men were local leaders in mechanisation, shedding labour and cutting costs and avoiding the pitfalls experienced by the Calcot establishment. But as their workers left for Mr Morris's car assembly plant in Oxford, more work fell on those who remained.

The Clarks were rigid non-conformists, representing a strong tradition in the Cotswold villages. Their extraordinary effort to survive was justified by their faith, which in turn justified their work. Father's descriptions of life with the Clarks, the interminable prayers, the scant rations and the expectation of effort remained with him always. Family visits to the two villages in the 1950s, which by then seemed to me miracles of modern farming presided over by a beneficent squirearchy, loosed in him childhood memories of exile from home, and conditions that were meant to "improve" him and make him a better person as well as a farmer. It cannot be surprising if some of his own attitudes to fatherhood were forged in these years. After the loneliness of his early years, brought up by the women of the previous generation, with little attention from either parent, and few companions of his own age, he had not made an auspicious start. The death of his father could have been the ultimate disaster.

Yet, in later life, he described it as a blessed relief. While his father was not exactly attentive in conventional modern terms, he was a stickler for what he regarded as the correct procedure. Once, watching my children eating soup, Father remarked that at their age, if he had eaten his soup from the near side rather than the far side of the bowl he would have been sent from the table and not fed again until the next day. His father was clearly a martinet in small matters, in an age when showing outward affection to small children was regarded either as unmanly or likely to spoil them. Despite the cold days at the Clarks, despite the other exile of being sent away to school, the death of his father was a release.

Chapter 12

A Visit to Paradise

THE LEAST RELIABLE of our unreliable witnesses was my grandmother. This is not to say that she invented things, but she certainly had a firm idea of how matters should have proceeded and the more times she told the stories the more closely they approximated to what should have occurred. When we no longer had her in our midst, and her death was the first major mortality in our close family that I experienced, we were bereft of a vibrant and determined figure of huge willpower. In retrospect, we may even have lost a type of truth teller, one who respected nobody's feelings and always called out her version of events, regardless of the consequences.

She was not happy in a feminine world of tea tables and gossip – she had to be with men (no less gossipy) and even in late middle age the photographs of Jane's or Mary's weddings show her diminutive figure, tightly attached to the arm of a compliant man to whom she had taken a shine. In other relationships she could be repetitively critical, especially to and about her immediate family and while her love for her children and their offspring was a given, she sometimes found it hard to remember to express it. While my maternal grandmother was always pulling me aside for a hug, or to covertly pass over a small coin or a chocolate bar, such largesse would be unthinkable in Gran Worlock. But she was hugely entertaining in other ways.

If we slip back into 1955, when she was still a very powerful force, we would have been careful not to speak out of turn. Hearing her rapid footsteps on the paving stones outside the front door at Nibley Farm on a day when she was expected could be enough to create a feeling that careful, if not best, behaviour was now required. The footsteps were followed by the very energetic banging of the great circular metal knocker on the front door.

"Go and let your grandmother in," came my mother's slightly anxious voice from the kitchen, as she prepared the pheasants which, once on the table in an hour or so, would invite comparisons with meals Gran had eaten at other Worlock tables, or even pheasants properly prepared by her own mother-in-law at Tresham.

I race to the door. It is big and heavy but I only have it open a fraction before a familiar voice chides,

"Are you all dead or asleep in there? I have been standing here for years and years and donkey's years, and if I have caught a fever in the process then you will be to blame for finishing me off! Now, what do you say? Don't mumble! Do you have a father or a mother at home – I need to speak to someone I can understand?"

As I take in the embattled warrior on the doorstep, I hear my mother's voice from the kitchen:

"David, pull up Gran's chair to the fireplace so she can get warm. Then hang up her coat and get her a glass of Amontillado."

And as Boudicca sweeps past me, flattening me back into the door with a metaphorical chariot wheel, I take stock of the awesome figure now standing in the hallway. She is a little over five feet tall, a stocky figure made to seem more substantial by what she is wearing. The huge musquash fur coat removes a regular sense of the wearer's shape. It is a present from two of her sons, like the television in the vast box with the postcard-sized screen bought for the 1953 Coronation. These gifts, which carry status as well as love, mark an acknowledgement that she, and she alone, carried them through the uncertainties and insecurities of the 1920s and 1930s into these calmer postwar waters and into relative prosperity.

I step forward to take the impossibly heavy coat, and as she opens it I am swept away on the heady odour of Lilies of the Valley. And as I struggle to hang the coat (now the smell is only of mothballs) Gran gets to work on detaching the fox fur from around her neck. It is a full fur: the fox's head and open mouth are used to create the site for the catch, whose other end is on the animal's bushy tail. The catch is difficult: I know when to be patient and silent. After the fox we come to the hat. It is a dark purple felt cloche, worn at a rakish angle. It is secured through the hair by a long pin: she has a variety of these, and today's has on the top end a large white round stone.

As she hands both hat and pin to me she says, "Pearl almost as big as a gull's egg – gift of a gentleman admirer."

She always says that, and I always nod, though it will be a good few years before I know what either of these statements mean, or that neither is quite right.

But one day in my tenth year she makes a different entrance. She has come not to eat dinner and set our world to rights, but to collect me along with my cousin Rob who is staying with us, and take us … on a visit. And we are just a bit apprehensive. For one thing, we have never been anywhere with her before, without our parents. Then, again, she had made this visit conditional on our displaying our very best behaviour. She made it clear that we were about to be judged by the very highest standards. She said she was determined not to be disgraced by us but if we did misbehave then we should never be forgiven, or "inherit", whatever that meant. However, it was tinged with fear in our minds.

The previous week, while playing on her back lawn behind the little bungalow in Downend to which she had retired, we had thrown a tennis ball hard enough to break her bathroom window. It was a small frosted window and some in our family said it had been cracked already and just fell out when the ball hit it, but whatever the truth of the matter we boys were a bit scared. Could this be Gran's punishment? She had been surprisingly nice at the time, ignoring us and telling my mother that she was not surprised, that Rob and I were the spoilt children of indulgent parents and she expected nothing less than Father having the window repaired at his own expense.

However, when news of the planned visit became known we got a good deal of family encouragement. Father laughed sarcastically and said we would learn a lot if we kept our eyes open. In fact we would see things that he and the rest of the family would never see. My mother was equally encouraging, saying we were like family ambassadors and were responsible for building better relationships. But decisively, sisters Mo and Mary complained that only boys were allowed to go and see these things. This reaction settled it for us. Whatever dreadful things lay in store for us, we were going with Gran to see ... Paradise.

Time perhaps now for a little background so that you can appreciate the magnitude of this announcement. Gran, particularly after the death of her husband and then her daughter (Father would interject here, "managed like a scullery maid and worked as hard as any servant") felt a driving need to manage the lives and destinies of her sons. This took many forms. One was her insistence that Father, seen as a proficient judge and dealer in cattle, should be the livestock buyer for the family. John, at last getting the ducal nod and becoming a Badminton tenant, should accept Father's purchases, and their prices. Not unnaturally the younger brother thought he could do better and the umbrage taken when it was demonstrated that he couldn't, marked a coolness between the brothers that lasted into their middle age. But in the early years, as the young men grew more self-willed, it must have become clear to Gran that she needed allies. A part of this management had to be accomplished through the women they married – which meant in turn that she had to approve of and be sure she could work with these women.

In the 1930s it would have been unlikely that the young men would have married without that approval. Her position as a strong and controlling matriarch made it impossible. But the marriages as they emerged must have seemed hugely unlikely. All of the boys were shy and introverted to a degree. No one could have imagined Father, awkward and without social graces and conversation, going to a Beetle Drive (a dice game which rewarded the first to score enough to put the parts on a beetle body) and coming back with a city girl from Bristol.

The party, at nearby Pucklechurch, was a charity event organised by friends of Gran. She sent her eldest to represent her and because he "never gets out". Another family attending the same event brought their daughter and her girlfriend who was staying with them. She was smart and ambitious, the assistant legal secretary to W. G. Scammell, the senior partner at Burges Salmon, then as now the leading agricultural law practice in the city of Bristol.

She was the daughter of a merchant seaman who went to work on the sailing vessels out of Avonmouth in his earliest teens, then moved to dry land as a Cotswold police constable, a springboard to a career as a detective which saw him become Gloucestershire's first Detective Chief Inspector. Like her two elder brothers, she was aspirational and driven, at once mindful of the lowly status, in her mind, of her innkeeper grandfather and the need to mix with the right people, like her friends in the hockey club. Did she gel with Gran the first time she heard Gran intone "keep yourself up"?

Gran must have seen the young woman's growing devotion to her son: it became a mutual bonding based on trust and loyalty and, eventually on his part, an acceptance of a management as complete as ever his mother had exercised. But this was yet to come: in those early exchanges after the Beetle Drive, Gran clearly saw something that she wanted on board. She knew Father needed managing. Like his father he could become possessed of an idea, suffer delusions of grandeur amongst other things, or plunge in one direction without examining the options. Gran became convinced that Kath would keep him straight. Advice may have been imparted: "give him his hunting and he will be easier to manage" or "keep a grip on the actual financial situation" (my mother became the farm book-keeper for the rest of her life).

After the marriage, Gran clearly had confidence in the management scheme she had approved. Kath became an expert in the kitchen and, under Gran's tutelage, someone who could prepare a brace of pheasants or a loin of venison in the approved manner. And if they spoilt their children? The relationship turned into a strong bond in which both women could speak freely. After the marriage Gran moved out of Nibley Farm and into a neighbouring house in the village, and then into a bungalow thirteen miles away.

Though satisfactory, this was only one of the three management dispositions that Gran needed to make. Her second son, John, she described as "moody", and Father called him an "uncooperative dreamer". In old age we chatted amicably enough, but there were still traces of a reserve, an unwillingness to talk about personal things (that definition could include milk production figures) that reflected generational attitudes and a reluctance in country villages to say more about anything than strictly needed to be said. But it also betrayed another trait, strong in this family: a fear of inviting criticism. Parents with sharp tongues, grandparents measuring progress towards agricultural competence against the template of previous generations, siblings quick to humble any boast: this was not a family that invited extrovert behaviour and John did not display any.

Yet there was a shy and secretive charm there. This was not the man without qualities that Father sometimes portrayed. As a tenant farmer at Bushes Farm, Horton, he had a mixed holding on a shelf of land between Sodbury Vale and the Cotswold escarpment. The inescapable mix of milking, grazing and some store cattle formed his farming practice. The village was famous for its Manor House, in which Tyndale produced the first vernacular version of the Bible. That activity would have meant certain death in Catholic England, but it can hardly have been kept more secret than John's farming or domestic activities. The brothers did not visit and neither did their families. John's shy charm was not exercised on them, but it did bring him one of Gran's most lofty aspirations – an heiress as a bride. Marry an heiress and you re-insure against the dreadful insecurities of wheat prices falling or markets crashing. You would put up with a lot to net an heiress.

So Gran was in the mood to be accommodating to Marge, the only child of wealthy Vale landowners and stewards of the Duke's lower woodlands. Gran said, "after all, she is a Limbrick" with exactly the same emphasis as she used on her own family name. Limbricks and Hatheralls, we understood, were just a cut above the Worlocks. She explained to the rest of us that Marge could have done better, had in fact married "down". She was a person of real artistic refinement. Her clothes came from the best shops in Bath or Bristol or Cheltenham. She had "taste", and that was something farmer's wives so rarely had. But she was certainly not just a farmer's wife, and to prove it the interior of Bushes Farm was ripped out and remodelled into a place where the gentry might be entertained. Marge adhered to "keep yourself up", and indeed she was "up" already.

So was Gran able to manage Marge as in the earlier years she had sought to manage and instruct my mother? It seems unlikely. Marge saw the whole Worlock ménage as social inferiors. She did not want them traipsing through her house or consorting with her delicate son, Richard. Even Gran's visits were demoted from a week in the guest room to periodic visits for lunch. And the Bushes Farm Worlocks, who never invited us to theirs, were never seen at our table. Gran became the sole pipeline of communication, and she was not a reliable witness. She probably exacerbated the issues between the households in the tales she carried between them.

The story became even more complex when her youngest son, Dick, the "Peach", married the girl who came to the farm to collect and record the milk samples for testing. This needs a place of its own, since it introduces my favourite aunt, the wonderful Joyce Grindon. Anyway, we are about to set out on a visit, and Gran is impatient to get going.

And Gran certainly had the full attention of Cousin Robert and myself that morning in 1955 when she ushered us out of the front door at Nibley, across the main road and into line at the bus stop adjacent to the Swan. We were about to go "where no man had gone before". Well, no Worlock man or woman certainly. We are armed with indoor shoes in bags: Marge has sent instructions that no one will be admitted wearing outdoor shoes. We are excited. Gran seems to have forgotten her bathroom window and is giving us a lecture on the importance of cousinhood.

We are the three male cousins, she is saying, and we must stick together and support each other since we will each take over his father's farm, and will need all the help we can get. Looking back I fully taste the irony of her effort to secure in the next generation what had been missed in the previous one. At the time, I surmise that I would just have felt that empty desperation that I always felt when this assumption about my farming future came into the conversation. I could see that this was not the case with Cousin Robert, and, despite the fact that I had never met him, I rashly assumed that Cousin Richard, six years older than me, was another committed child farmer.

But Gran is on edge. When the green single-decker arrives, bound for Chipping Sodbury via Yate, she asks the driver for a single and two halves. With almost ritual truculence and looking at us he responded,

"So how old are they?"

Through gritted teeth she spat back: "Halves."

We stood on the steps for a long moment until he had taken a good look at Gran, four square and embattled behind a wall of musquash. Did he catch the eye of the fox? In any event he just issued the tickets, and we went in and climbed into our seats.

Gran sat in front and we sat on the seat behind her. It took twenty-five minutes to crawl up through Yate – I pointed out to Rob each of the five educational establishments I had so far attended in my first five years of educational life – until we reached Sodbury clock tower, where we changed buses for one marked "Hawkesbury Upton via Horton".

Now Gran sat behind us, issuing instructions as to behaviour and the importance of not bringing dirt or germs into the house. Richard was very susceptible to infection, which was why this meeting of cousins could not take place at Nibley, which was thought to be a hotbed of infection. Above all, "Don't ask questions, just answer them!" I had a distinct impression that Gran was nervous – and by the time she had finished so were we.

The bus left us in the centre of Horton village by the cross-roads and we walked up muddy lanes until we reached the farm. Uncle John was certainly a much tidier farmer than Father. No rusting farm implements strewn across the yards here. The approach to the thatched farmhouse was immaculate – not exceptional today in barn-conversion Britain, but wholly strange in 1955. If Father was an advocate of the "where there's muck there's money" school, Bushes Farm clearly lay in Gentleman Farmer territory. We poor cousins were impressed as Gran gave an imperious rat-a-tat of the door knocker.

While we waited, Gran indicated that we should get our shoes off, and we were in the process of changing in the porch when the door opened, and the mistress of the house appeared. Our street shoes were to be left in the porch and our clean shoes, carefully scrubbed by my mother, were inspected and deemed clean enough for admittance. And so we entered the world of Paradise.

Marge said, by way of greeting,

"We'll have lunch in the kitchen, because I don't want them (here a suspicious glance at Rob and me) spilling things in my dining room."

And Gran responded,

"Well, Marge, just show them your sitting room, I always tell the family that it is as close as any of us will get to Paradise!" Flattery opened doors and, halfway down the corridor a door was flung open and we paused to take in the effect.

We gazed into … what seemed to a ten-year-old boy to be just another sitting room. Rob was about to walk in when his hostess placed a cautionary hand on his shoulder. We were allowed to look, but not enter. I recall two huge Ming vases, as tall as I was, on either side of the fireplace. Rob asked about the strange flowers coming out of them, only to be told that they were ostrich feathers … I asked about the little embroidered bibs on the back of each chair. "Antimacassars" came the response. I did not sort this out until I told my mother that several Paradise items belonged to Aunt Marge's Aunty. By this time our hostess had realised that, as an audience, her nephews were not worth the trouble. We were hurried into the kitchen, Cousin Richard and lunch.

Richard was tall and pale, and had nothing in common with his visitors. When I met him again at weddings and funerals, I didn't recognise him. I can remember his mother saying that he didn't have farmer's hands because I looked guiltily at my own. Was it so instantly recognisable? But my chief memory of that lunch was Gran, having told us that we were the heirs and successors of a proud line of Worlock farmers all born to farm, she needed to explain to us why we had all been named and christened as we were.

She pointed out that the eldest son of the eldest son was always named Robert. The name was lucky. Non-Robert eldest sons in the past had been punished for cattle rustling or sheep stealing or a variant on agriculture's traditional capital crimes. But no Robert had suffered this fate, so as a protective measure the eldest son of the eldest son was and would be for ever Robert.

So, Gran drew in her breath and proceeded, after a sharp glance at her daughter-in-law,

"Richard is the son of my second son, John, and is named for my third son, my Peach. So he could not be Robert."

"And no one will ever call him Dick while I am alive," said his mother.

"And you, Rob," Gran continued, "were christened Robert, because after my son Robert, David's father, had three girls I gave up hope, and 1944 was a difficult year, so I insisted that you were christened Robert Winston. Then I knew that the tradition would go on, so it was a surprise, David, when you came along, the eldest son of the eldest son, but the Robert name was gone. So we christened you David Robert."

As this story unfolded I can recall a cascade of emotions. What an immensely powerful person Gran is, naming us all and deciding our destinies. Then, so if I missed out on the name, does this explain why I really don't want to be a farmer? Does *not* having the name excuse me from dedicating my life to farming? And if it does, why does everyone else, especially Father and Gran, continue to talk as if my farming life was inevitable?

Soon it was time to return, and face the barrage of questions from my family. And I held it over them for the rest of their lives. I remain the only one who ever peeped around the door of Paradise.

Chapter 13

A Joycean Digression

G RAN'S DESK has always been a good place to think
and work. Its worn surface, warped and ill-fitting
drawers and the desk furniture I always remember –
the onyx slab with the stag's horns and the silver-mounted
monthly adjustable calendar – are able to conjure up 1955 in
a moment. It came to me when she died but did she leave it to
me, or did my mother think I needed a desk? It has stuck to me
ever since, too small and oddly ugly, but as I try to reconstruct
the crucible of my childhood, the decision not to be a farmer,
it seems almost like a witness.

Did Gran sit here and think about how she ran a business
and a family and a love life? Were the decisions made here

which arguably starved her eldest son of affection, and in turn made it so difficult for him to form a relationship with his own son? Yet in so many ways Gran and Father were just enacting the rituals of family relationships common to their age and the prevalent beliefs of society around them. Like all of us, they were doing this with an eye on the practices of the past and without any precognition of the speed of social change and the increased range of aspirations that marked the world they were emerging into after 1945.

Yet there can be no doubting the power of Gran in all our relationships. As she voyaged between the households of her three sons she incited critical passions on all sides. She had done this in their boyhood, she did it amongst their wives, and she worked on their children in the same way. In the latter category we all suffered, but one's own sufferings always seem sharper. Did anyone know, she would ask the dinner table, why I had failed the eleven-plus exam and Rob had got into the King's School, Gloucester? And how was it that one brother's son was a perfect helper to his father and the other was work shy and a poor prospect in farming terms? Rob got the same treatment in reverse. Had Gran's sons received the same treatment in their childhoods? If so, did they resent Dick the Peach, the youngest boy and the only one who could do right?

Except that in one respect he had not done right. He had married Joyce Grindon, my beloved and favourite aunt. On the surface this could not be faulted. Her social standing was impeccable, both because she was the daughter of the local magis-trate, and because with her outgoing and vivacious character, she seemed to have an endless circle of friends.

"Joyce knows everyone, and everyone's business," Gran would sigh. And then: "I suppose she would, traipsing round the farms picking up milk samples."

"Milk samples" in this context could be enunciated to make it sound like a socially transmittable disease. Most of all, she must have appeared to her mother-in-law as a very suitable case for treatment. Gran took to spending two or more weeks at a time at the farm at Westbury-on-Severn once her youngest son was established there. Then it was the birth of the children. Gran become a vital component of household life and the instructor of another daughter-in-law.

But both of her other daughters-in-law had a little more protection, either through experience in professional life or via private wealth. Joyce was younger, with a strong orientation towards a packed social life, like Gran herself, but a wonderful passive resistance towards instruction in matters culinary or childcare. When Gran reported that Rob wouldn't eat and was being raised on bread, gravy and custard (without lumps) the rest of the family were intended to be scandalised and Joyce abashed. But we were not scandalised. We all knew that Gran was sharpening a knife for each of us:

"It's time Jane got married – it's pointless sending her to Agriculture college."

"I made Jane and Mo what they are by persuading Robert to send them to boarding school – otherwise Kath would have spoilt them."

"They should have sent Mary too – too shy to open her mouth."

My mother had a sympathy for Joyce born out of shared experience. Perhaps it was this that decided her on the idea of exchanging children in the long summer holidays. In effect this meant initially that I got to go to Westbury for a couple of weeks each summer, since both sister Mary and Cousin Robert were too homesick to travel. After a while Robert became an exchange cousin too, and since neither of us had a huge following of local friends (my mother despaired of finding "suitable" – socially acceptable – friends in the village or the locality) we became good company for each other. And home-sickness was never my issue, in this instance or later at boarding school, being beyond the constant pressure to be the farmer's son Father expected, or the daily supplications from my mother as she tried to please us all by saying,

"Now I know your father is working alone this morning on laying the hedge in Sixteen Acres – he would be so happy if you went out and helped."

This was now the normal precursor to Father's "So you want to help? Well, have I got a job for you ...!" routine. If I was at Westbury, just as later when I was at school, I was away from a cycle which could only end in disappointment and recriminations all round.

Joyce understood this from the beginning. She provided a space without pressure. She was one of the most naturally friendly and outgoing people that I have ever met. Her curiosity and naturalness meant that she could ask questions that others feared to pose, and find her level with people of all sorts immediately. But what she spotted about me was the one thing which no one in my own home had seemingly recognised. After a few days of that initial holiday, she said,

"You would be just as happy if we let you read a book for as long as you liked."

I sighed with relief.

Next day she returned from Gloucester with a huge family saga novel that she found on the remainder shelf at W. H. Smith. It was called *The Mill on the Po*, by Ricardo Bacchielli, and I started it after breakfast the following day. I finished just before dinner. No one said I had to do something. It was a heavenly day. It was also the beginning of something else.

Like my mother's two clever brothers, who went to Bristol Grammar School, and then passed their insurance and accountancy examinations to become professionals, I seemed to be able to read quickly and absorb what I read. From the age of ten I read like an auto-didact, self-educating by following my nose from the last book to the next. In my eighteenth year, at the zenith of this passion for self-improvement, I read and recorded the consumption of two hundred works of history, literary criticism, novels and plays.

Yet this had to be kept a secret, since Father's desire to be succeeded by a farming son had to be kept a possibility. Or so my mother believed. Did Father really believe it during these years? He certainly doubted it very publicly at times, to the extent that I felt I was playing two different roles. I could shed the bumbling excuse for a farmer's son at Westbury because it just did not matter to Joyce.

It helped that I was always a hearty eater. Joyce, under critical fire from her mother-in-law for cakes that sank in the middle, or frustrated by children who were fussy eaters, responded to my clean plate and enthusiasm for second helpings. And I responded to her wonderful spontaneity. She was a rare parent who could reshape the day in ten minutes after breakfast, scrap all previous plans and half an hour later be putting a picnic in the car for a day trip up into the mysterious delights of the Forest of Dean.

Perhaps this was because they were younger than my parents, and decidedly less ferocious than the previous generation. She was greatly distressed when, with Gran, we were visiting her parents at their house, Jordan Court, outside Westbury. It was plum season in the great orchards around the house and while wandering there I found a young pigeon with an injured wing. Catching it, I entertained the idea of keeping it in the hope it would get better, but Gran had other ideas.

"It's a pest," she stormed. "Drown it in that water butt."

"Quicker to do this," said old Mrs Grindon and, turning on me as I held the bird with its wings pinioned to its sides, she grasped its neck and with a practiced tug pulled its head right off. Great gouts of blood poured down me and scores of tiny feathers stuck to me. Joyce cleaned me up, and for the rest of the holiday asked about my dreams each morning.

Yet despite these reminders of an older generation, Joyce was a liberator, and in time I felt that I was myself at Westbury. The long lazy curve of the Severn's horseshoe bend signalled a place where I could be me, and my witty kindly uncle sensed this as well. One day he brought me his own handwritten journal from his two years as an itinerant farmworker in Australia to read. When I had finished it I asked him what had pushed him to this adventure of leaving the Cotswolds.

"Well," he said drily, "I was a young man working for your father, and he wasn't exactly easy to please. As you know, sometimes it's good to get away!"

And then he remarked shyly that none of his family knew he had written this journal: would I read it to them, a few pages after dinner each evening. At Westbury I was a different person, valued in a different way from the way in which Father saw me at home.

Chapter 14

Getting the Same Education

IN 1955, whether it was the threat to family or hunting that had the upper hand in Father's mind, we all agreed that it was a very wet year. Father and I were enacting our danse macabre of father–son relationships, though neither of us had ever heard of Edmund Gosse. Father had more on his mind than a stubborn and recalcitrant son who secretly knew he would never be a farmer; he was worried by the bills for cattle cake.

Our entire enterprise was now overwhelmingly dependent on the monthly milk cheque. Corn, cash crops, and cattle dealing were a drop in the revenue bucket alongside the milk. The sharply rising costs of feeding the cows, and the need to feed them well enough to get as much milk from them as we could, were contributing to a sense of crisis. The family insecurities around farming failure were never far away. The threat to his wife and young family exerted real pressure. So did the possibility, never realised even in the most severe circumstances, that he might have to reduce or suspend those two days a week spent following hounds.

Father believed passionately in the "Get Out Of Jail" card. Wherever they were, his grandmother and great-aunt would intercede with Providence. In this process he would come by the "big idea" which would resolve the current crisis and restore normality. So he waited – and the big idea came. Mangelwurzels! Had he not seen in a farm sale recently an ancient device that chopped root vegetables, at the turn of a handle, into chunks small enough to be eaten by a cow? Obtain one of those, grow the German chard cheaply, chop up its red, round roots and feed them to our cows and the bills from British Oil and Cake Mills (BOCM) would drop dramatically. Just as the crisis depression had been a little manic, so the solution euphoria became over-whelming. We planted the tiny mangel plants in backbreaking rows on the quite steep slopes of the field on the other side of our lower woods. Then we top dressed the field with nourishing dung from the cowsheds. Then we waited.

It was a very wet year. The dung was powerful and soon made everything grow, including the seeds from all the grasses eaten by the cows and passed through them. Bert Harford and his two sons leant on the gate and politely asked if we had anything under that weed bed. But we could not use a tractor and a hoe to clean things up. The field had moved from wet to muddy, too muddy for wheels. So we all got out there with hand hoes, and began the painfully slow job of cutting out the weeds and giving our little mangels a chance of survival.

But Father was a man of the pre-tractor world, and surely

in one of our piles of rusting and ancient equipment, we had
a horse hoe? Yes, we did, and soon Twist, the old cob, was
attached to it. This would speedily take out the weeds between
the rows of mangels, leaving the hand hoe people to take out
the weeds around the plants themselves. Father, at the back of
the horse hoe and holding its handles and with Twist's reins
around his neck, would show us how. The demonstrator, horse
and hoe readied themselves at the top of the field and then
plunged violently forward: the hoe addressed the soil, and, to
our onlooking horror, neatly took out a line of young mangels,
leaving a line of untouched weeds as evidence of the efficacy of
horse hoeing over useless tractors.

But we did not laugh. Bob and Nobby Williams. Chris
Hawkins. Paul Benjamin. Gerald Prendergast. The Boss's son.
Even old Fred Timbrell, though he had already had a glass
or two of cider. We knew better than to laugh. In the silence,
Father said that we had all better get back to hand hoeing,
but the boy could be spared to lead the horse and make sure
it went straight.

So off we set again, while five grown men tried to weed and
watch at the same time. On taking Twist by the halter it was
obvious to me that he hated the whole business as much as I
did. Father retained the reins, and steered the hoe. I tried to
get the horse to walk one side of the row of mangels while I
walked the other, but he always wanted to be on my side, with
his huge hooves scraping the back of my wellingtons. Every
time he did that I jumped out of the way. Looking over my
shoulder, I could tell that this gave us a motion of a small boat
on a choppy sea. The master mariner on the bridge at the back
of this unlikely agricultural equipage was also riding the waves,
but from his mouth came torrents of curses and reflections
on the pure uselessness of the son with whom he had been

handicapped. Looking down, I could see that the strange motion we had adopted down the field had neatly taken out every other mangel in the row.

Shortly after this I was sent back to the house either to find someone who could lead a horse in a straight line or never darken Father's doors again. I was ready for the latter, but my mother prevailed upon my sister Jane to help me and we returned to the field. With one on either side of the horse's head we persuaded the stubborn old cob to hold a direction, and finished that part of the job in the early evening. Then it rained again, and it went on raining. The mangels grew beautifully. Father should have got an award for the best crop of roots. But we still could not get on the land to harvest them. Nobby Williams got the tractor and trailer stuck, and when he tried to accelerate out of axle-deep mud that held the trailer, the tractor back-flipped. He was flung out of the side and broke his collarbone.

And still the mangels grew. Soon the field was my favourite on the farm, another Mato Grosso in which one could hide unseen. I cut staves and made swords from the huge mangel stalks, while the roots grew from cannon balls to beach balls. The field became an involuntary nature reserve until, at the end of the summer, we ploughed it all back into the soil.

"I do reckon that must be the best fertilised field on your farm," said Bert Harford, leaning on the gate. We took no notice. While we liked Bert and his sons, they were not the sort of people my mother would invite for dinner.

Anyway, it was 1956, and we needed to be saved all over again. This time the big idea did not come to Father as a brainwave: it came to Uncle Don, my mother's brother, and it was born of a soldier's experience ten years earlier. As a young lieutenant in the logistics branch of the Royal Army Service Corps, Don had run oil supplies to British tank regiments before evacuating at St Nazaire after the debacle of Dunkirk. Transferring to the Indian Army, he did the same for the vital supply lines out of Bombay across the continent to the Army fighting in Burma. Ending the war as a major, he returned to post-war employment with Shell Mex where he had been a pre-war trainee, and rose through the ranks there as easily as he had in the army. My mother loved him intensely since he had all the humour of their mother and none of the sententiousness of her father or elder brother.

So we paid great regard to what he said. In 1956, as noted above, he said a lot of things about the Suez Canal. While I was getting my first political education by gazing at the headlines on the racks of newspapers in Mr Lemon's shop and asking what these poor Arabs had done to be bombed and strafed and invaded other than try to raise their tolls, Don was telling Father, with increasing urgency, to gather up his savings, raise every bit of cash he could lay his hands on, and funnel it into a quoted company which would, in a short while, make our fortunes. None of this appealed to Father at all. He found his brother-in-law overfamiliar (the younger man addressed the elder as "Robbsie"), he was bored by interminable anecdotes of clubs and golf courses in which not a single horse ever appeared, and he had no interest in motor cars or labour-saving electrical devices in the home. In both of these areas Don was an expert and quite failed to understand why we were not taking advantage of them.

He had fought in a war and been through the Suez Canal twice, so he must know something. No Worlock, all in wartime reserved occupations, could match this. So when Don said the new magic which would save the Worlock fortunes was called Ultramar, a company that drew its oil exclusively from

Venezuela and Mexico, and when he said it was a gamble, but a good one, Father's eyes lit up. All his life he loved a risk, whether over the fences or in doing a deal. The normal restraint was his prudent and sensible wife. But here she was forced to be an advocate of risk, or undermine the credibility of the brother who could do no wrong. So we all went for Ultramar, hook, line and sinker.

In the pre–invasion of Suez period we noted odd, gentle movements in its share price. Then the shares were tipped by Patrick Sergeant, City Editor of the *Daily Mail*, later knighted for services to Lord Rothermere and faithfully followed thereafter by Father. Once the paratrooper attack had taken place, and enough shipping had been sunk in the canal effectively to render it useless to all of the combatants, my mother was watching for the newspaper each morning, and reporting the share price rises to Father at breakfast. He sought to adopt the demeanour of a seasoned investor, allowing no expression of surprise bar the occasional: "That man Sergeant certainly has his ears to the right doors!"

But when to sell and realise the profits? Neither Patrick Sergeant nor Don had anything useful to say on this point, which disturbed many a breakfast as the now plateauing share price worried the Nibley investment team. The slightest fall was seen as a certain "sell" signal, and the slightest rise as a sure sign that values were about to quadruple once again as they had done several times already. And then John Foster Dulles intervened and helped the investors properly to evaluate their risk position. When he, as US Secretary of State, said that the USA did not support the war aims of the invaders and would see that no one ran short of oil, the game was over. Father made the call and found himself in possession of the largest capital sum he had ever banked.

This sudden capital injection had two immediate effects. One was the quickening of the process by which, instalment by instalment, we were buying Nibley Farm. Two years later the process was complete, and Clifton Estates sent over a handsome deed of ownership, which I was invited to admire. Another step towards security. Another step away from failure. The first of Gran's sons to own his own farm. It was a huge moment, larger than I could ever have guessed at the time, even if the mortgage was still sizeable and onerous.

But it was the second element that slightly surprised me. My mother said that we could now afford to send me away to school. Until that moment I had never guessed there was a doubt on that score. I was always told that I would go away to school, the same school that my father and grandfather had attended. It would "sort me out" and "make a man of me" just as it had for him. Where he had failed, they would succeed: they would "knock some sense into me" and I would return to the farm a different person.

I had always rather looked forward to going away. It promised a suspension of hostilities with Father on the farmwork frontline. And in the year of Suez I failed my eleven-plus examination, leaving other, grammar school, bridges to higher education ablaze. But I had not fully realised that actually getting away and going to school had been facilitated by the last flicker of imperial powerlessness, that most immoral and unforgivable post-colonial folly, the Suez invasion.

Chapter 15

A Day at the Market

I T WAS EASY TO HATE Yate market. It was about two miles
from Nibley, squashed into the railway yard alongside the
station. A visit there often meant taking livestock up the
main road, with the risk of beasts bolting into treasured but
unprotected domestic gardens, or bringing them back unsold.
The curses of the aggrieved fell mostly on the child herds-
people who had to run in and bring them out, and not upon the
man on horseback who stayed out on the road. And if we were
buying, then the wanderings of our disorientated purchases,
after leaving their homes and being herded around sales rings
all day, were even worse.

Then there were the days when I too was herded, into the

demon barber's shop of Les Scuse, haircutter and town tattooist. Waiting one's turn, the images of dragons and sampans allowed you to imagine emerging like Fu Manchu, a "yellow peril" sent to terrorise the nearby council house estates. Les, the grinning genius of the place, dressed only in vest and trousers, sweating profusely onto his customers as he shaved around the heads of a dozen small boys, leaving a clump of hair on top which would not have disgraced a mangelwurzel. Les was the image of exactly what you didn't want to see approaching delicate skin with a sharp needle or an open razor.

Was it the three or four yellowing teeth that emerged with his smile or the ash-dropping cigarette that hovered over you precariously from his lower lip while he worked? Or his feeble and repetitive jokes? He always asked me, at the age of ten, if I wanted "something for the weekend", causing gales of laughter amongst his waiting clients while reminding the adults that this was where you bought your condoms. On market day he was always full. As a result of his education I have never had a tattoo, and from adulthood always insisted on having my hair cut by women.

But there were other markets, and trips to Gloucester were to be relished. No risk here of being cursed for my stupidity, since we were always in the company of other men, several of whom, like the elderly cattle dealer, Joe Roach, were very kind to me. Not only were we on our best behaviour but in our best clothes. Father adorned for Gloucester Market was a sight akin to Father going hunting. Nothing too extraordinary about the shirt with its stiff, white detached collar, bow tie held in place by a tiepin under the bow, since the bow tie was the real thing. The upper part was completed with a bright yellow waistcoat with brass buttons. Glance down, and you see a man in jodhpurs, his calves protected by stiff leather spats. Each side of these leggings was comprised of thirty tiny buttons, done up with a button hook worked lovingly by sister Mary, kneeling on the floor beside the great man. Last of all came highly polished brown boots. Add a stick (the thumb stick will do nicely for pushing cattle around a sales ring) and a hat (choice of a bowler or perhaps the broad-rimmed brown homburg) and we are complete. But, remember, no real man goes anywhere without a hat.

So are we ready to go now? Not quite. There are two issues to be encountered when going anywhere with Father. He does not carry a watch or timepiece, and he does not have a purse or wallet or carry anything to do with money. Indeed he never carries money with him in any form at all. How this began I do not know. Did his mother not trust him with money? Going out as a family my mother carried cash and chequebook and supplied either on demand. These two things he has sworn have never proved to be a disadvantage to him. If pressed about time he would reply,

"But any damn fool can look at the sky and tell the time."

Here was yet another of my inadequacies in 1955, for I couldn't. Years later I was to understand that his guesses and mine equalled each other in accuracy, but for now, since neither of us had a watch, I had to rely on the certainty of his pronouncements after staring at the horizon – "It's between 3.30 and 4."

But the money was a different matter. Here I had an important role to play. The last act of leaving the house was my mother fiddling around with my jacket and handing it to me. After a while I knew what she was doing. Then she handed me two half-crowns to put in my pocket.

"They are for drinks and anything else that comes up."

She dropped us at the station and paid for our train tickets, and soon we were flitting away through Charfield and Wickwar, making all speed for Dursley, then into Stonehouse by the light industry park – "Is that where you are going to school?" joked Joe Roach – until we passed Quedgeley and it was time to gather up our things to alight at Gloucester. Then I patted that inside pocket: all was safe. The envelope was still secured to the jacket by the nappy pin, and inside it I could feel what I knew was an unsigned cheque, and a folded £20 note – in those days a white sheet the size of a small pocket handkerchief.

Years later I asked my parents about these strange happenings. Father, as always, said that he didn't carry money because he did not wish to eat and drink with anyone who wouldn't give him credit. This was feasible – a favourite maxim was that "a day spent more than five miles from my front door is a day wasted" – and certainly publicans and shopkeepers in his own vicinity would recognise him. But where did this aversion to carrying money begin? In his mother's aversion to the gambling and drinking habits of her husband or brothers? Was Father to be kept safe by being kept penniless? If so, he turned privation to advantage, and while he was a generous man when it came to paying his share or his round, there was always someone there with the necessary liquidity to cover the cost. Specifically on the envelope in the jacket pocket, my mother's reaction to being asked why she did it was to cover it in humour:

"Well, I wanted to make sure he brought you back." An ironic joke too, considering that at the age of five I had been lost in Gloucester – by my mother.

And so we, the Yate crowd, roll out of the station and down the street to the old Gloucester market, right in the city centre. The train journey, full of noise and stops and belching grey steam and black-grey smoke had seemed an epic of modern travel that had lasted all day. As an adult I know that it took twenty-seven minutes and we had covered twenty-four miles.

Such was the time and distance involved that I was ready for lunch, and I knew that I was not to be disappointed. My only concern was which of the two hostelries in the street would be chosen. The landlord of the Bell disliked children in bars and made me sit in the draughty porch. Here I had to rely on Father's haphazard memory for food and drink, and the memory became more intermittent as whisky was taken and stories of cattle-dealing derring-do were exchanged. But in the old Grosvenor Hotel I was allowed into the lounge bar, and could eat, drink and listen in the warm.

"What will the boy have?"

"Ham sandwich, plenty of mustard, packet o' crisps and a ginger beer," said Father.

"Likes his mustard?" said Joe Roach.

"I dunno," said Father, "but he will never be a man if he can't take mustard, beer and tobacco. No one likes them at first, you just have to get used to them."

I never had a problem with any of these things, but in recollection I see this was not about me, but someone else's difficult childhood being replayed in mine.

But we must drink up and hurry or we will miss the start of the big show. I slip Father the necessary warm coins and he pays. The bells in the two sale rings are sounding as we leave the warm, fuggy bar and engage with the bracing marketplace. Bellowing cattle, distraught at losing offspring. The steamy smell of freshly deposited cow dung. The clamour of a crowd dividing between the two venues. Are you a follower of Mr Stanley Bruton of Bruton Knowles and Sons? Then turn to your right. On the left side, and where we are heading, cows are sold by Mr Critchley Pope, of J. Pearce Pope and Sons. And there he is, just mounting the auctioneer's stand. Our hero, the little Napoleon, the pocket battleship himself.

"No one can sell a cow like Critch," we have said with certainty in the bar. "Gets the best prices in the market, that's certain sure."

We avow a fact which is impossible to verify, and which disguises the fact that our choice of an auctioneer is as rational as our loyalty to Bristol Rovers or Bristol City. You are born one way or the other. It's just the way we are.

Our man does not disappoint. Look at Critch now, chatting away from under the rim of the grey bowler hat to his two clerks, who stand either side of him with the ledgers and the gavel. Confidence is his cologne. As I stand on my toes and strain to see I know that his shining Bristol sports car will be in the private parking space behind the ring. I know he is waiting for the crowd to settle, for the theatrical moment of expectation, until he can smell what he needs to smell – readiness to buy cattle!

Meanwhile we fix our eyes on him, we take in the smiling blue eyes beneath the grey bowler, the determined chin held up by the cravat and the winged collar. Beneath the cravat, itself secured by a pearl pin (which looks the size of a pullet's egg from here), the gold brocade waistcoat and the half hunter across it are shown off by the plain, light-grey jacket. Unseen below the parapet are grey trousers and highly polished patent-leather shoes. This is a man dressed for theatre, and as a hush falls, the curtain goes up.

But the gathering concentration is broken by a latecomer. Pulling on a brown smock as he hurries in, the dealer nods at Critch as he takes his place.

"Come from a warm bed, eh, Johnston?" the auctioneer queries.

The dealer smiles, nods, looks round apologetically.

"But not his wife's! What do you think, gentlemen?"

And all we gentlemen bellow, "Not his wife's!"

And we are away. Now we are a group who, in three hours time, at the end of the performance, will be making those responses without a cue from Critch. Now he turns to a massive figure, bearded to the waist, who stands by the ring gate.

"First Lot: Baron," and that worthy opens the gate to admit three milking Friesians. The Red Baron moves them around the ring with his stick, helped from the sidelines by the poking, prodding, beating sticks of other dealers. Did the Baron really leave St Petersburg in 1917 for this? Who knows? Critch is starting.

"Property of Harford, Two Pools Farm. You all know him as a good 'un. Three Barreners, genuine article, who will start me, I need fifty…?" And thus the rapid-fire bidding commences. And ends.

"Down to Williams…" – Side of mouth to clerk: "Fourth row, haircut."

"Nice trim, Mr Williams – wedding, christening, funeral?"

And in three hours we will greet every market day haircut with that same question, at the direction of our conductor, compère, host and auctioneer. Sometimes it all goes wrong. The conductor's baton seeks an instrument not present in today's orchestra. When the gavel comes down, nothing is there.

"Down to scratch," rasps Critch to the clerk.

One day I ask Joe Roach who Mr Scratch is, and get a patient smile in return.

"You watch carefully, young 'un. Those cows were not sold at all. He sought a higher bid by pretending he already had the lower one, and when it wasn't forthcoming he bought the beast hisself. Watch now, you will see those lots come round again at the end. They go for a lower price then, so it's a drink in the private bar and an arm round the shoulder for that farmer, p'raps a bunch of flowers for the missus. Promises to put his stock up front next week, and not sell them when market enthusiasm is going down. Anything to stop the man going over the way to Brutons."

Eventually there are no more lots to be ushered in or out by the Baron. Critch brings matters to an end by a blow not of the gavel, but his silver-topped black cane on the woodblock. Dazed and disorientated cattle are being loaded with blows and kicks into unfamiliar vehicles. If we have bought we ride home in the cab of the cattle truck. If we have sold then we return by train, and if we did not get the price we wanted this can be a silent passage on Father's part. I am less concerned since the gossiping dealers and farmers are hugely interesting and entertaining to me, and the gossip always centres on our galvanic auctioneer.

"You 'eard how he had drunk so much after the sale at Berkeley Road that when he climbed into the Bristol he fell asleep before he could reach the controls …"

"When did he come to?"

"In the morning, apparently, and he was so stiff when they took him out they had to rub his limbs with five-star French brandy!"

"Well, I heard Critch and some of his cronies was drinking at the Hare and Hounds at Westonbirt and got to betting and Critch said that Bristol was so fast that he could drive it down the Tetbury road and go straight across the crossroads without looking either way on the main road, and if he were doing more than ninety he would be perfectly safe. And he did it to prove it!"

Thus we stitched and embroidered the lineaments of a "character" in the age before mass access to television and soap operas: our black-and-white, two-channel set at Nibley Farm in fact arrived that year.

But we did not know what made Father so angry when Critch undersold his cattle. We did know that Critch and Gran were old friends, that the two often had supper together, and that the sleek, black Bristol could be seen parked outside the bungalow, and some of us thought how natural that was, since Critch was Gran's brother-in-law, having married Gran's vivacious sister, Kath. We knew Kath had suffered a complete mental collapse and had died some years later, and all we knew about poor Kath came from Gran's other, younger sister, the kindly and outgoing Aunt Lil. She told us that, at the time of her collapse, Kath grew very worried that the Midland Bank would rob her of her money and valuables during the day, while staff were in the bank. When it was all locked up after hours, she was happy. Accordingly she went to the branch first thing in the morning and withdrew everything, then returned at closing to redeposit her treasures. Between these visits, and while Critch was selling cattle, she rode around Gloucester in the cab of a Vulture waste-disposal vehicle whose crew she had befriended, and who had formed such an affection for her that they picked her up and dropped her off at the appropriate places each day.

Father knew this and a bit more, and it fuelled his annoyance when he felt that Critch had not secured for us the best prices of the day. He knew that in those tough years after 1918, when he was a teenager with no father, Critch was the man Gran had reached out to for "comfort" and "solace". Not the only one, but a principal one. What this did for her sister's state of mind we do not know or speculate.

And Father, in later years, would simply say, "…Well, she always had to have a man in tow."

Critch was in no sense a role model or father figure and, indeed, in these years Father was boarded out in various places and then sent away to school. Did he resent the exuberant auctioneer? I can recall no evidence of that, but at least I know that he felt that the man had a moral obligation to secure the best prices available.

Chapter 16

"Creeping like Snail, Unwillingly to School"

ERE WE COME to a "fact", the sort of a fact that may have every significance for a story of this type, or which may simply have no significance at all. The fact is that Father, like his father, and like myself, went to the same school. Seventy years passed between Robert Thomas starting at Wycliffe College and David Robert leaving, a life expectancy in 1893 when Robert Thomas joined, but not a huge amount of time in the greater scheme of things.

Naturally, though, the school had changed radically in that time. It was founded in 1882 by a disappointed man. G. W. Sibley had been second master at Taunton School during his father's headmastership, but was not appointed when his father died.

He moved north to a town called Stonehouse, five miles from the old woollen town of Stroud in the Golden Valley, still in those years producing guardsmen's uniforms and billiard-table baize in faint remembrance of England's first medieval sheep-inspired industrial revolution, created by Cotswold farmers and their livestock. He bought the Haywardsfield Hall Estate, which contained two houses large enough to contain boys as boarders. One became the School House, and the other Haywardsfield. All three Worlocks, and Cousin Richard, who also went to Wycliffe, attended Haywardsfield.

So here is a constant: we all experienced the same building, and from that building we all looked at the same view. The blue line of the Cotswold escarpment is the backdrop of every view from the school buildings, connecting three hills – Frocester, Selsley and Rodborough Common – with Minchinhampton in a line that runs from Dursley in the south to Stroud in the north. All of the weather experienced in the vale beneath them was first written on these three hills, so I am certain that my father and grandfather glanced up at them as often as I did, anticipating sun or fearful of rain. Across these hills, starting in the village with Doverow hill, I walked and, when so compelled, ran. And so, I fondly imagine, did they.

There seem few other parallels to be drawn between these school experiences. The Sibley family were strong Methodists and this was the religious tradition of the school at its foundation, though by the 1960s it had declared itself to be ecumenical and undenominational. This is perhaps a clue to something else which permeated each of us. The school had none of the traditions or pretensions of the host of public-school foundations in the second half of the nineteenth century. There is no evidence here of the influence of Thomas Arnold. We were not educated to be Muscular Christians, incited to "play up, play up, and play the game", or intended to supply the manpower needs of Empire. Rather, I think, the school and the Sibleys – the founder's son, W. A. Sibley was still active in running it when I arrived – had less lofty ambitions. Their object was to inculcate a wider liberal education to meet the needs of lower-middle-class families. The children of professionals, managers, shopkeepers and farmers, of whom we had a great number. The non-conformist background was in tone with this and also allowed some unusual features: the school developed a house for vegetarians, a strong Sibley interest. Above all it should be local. Father and his father faced a twelve-mile journey from Tresham, while my own, twenty-two miles from Nibley, was hardly transcontinental.

Educational fashion and practice had changed radically in those seventy years, and ideas of how much education you might need, or could afford, are a useful indicator. Robert Thomas got two years, from age 14 to 16. Father arrived in 1921 and left in 1925, spending the ages of 13 to 17 on an education that he valued hugely. I followed him in 1956, finally departing in 1963, after seven years from the ages of 11 to 18, for which I owe grateful thanks to Gamal Abdul Nasser, Ultramar Oil and Uncle Don.

It is hard now to piece together the motivation for sending Robert Thomas away to boarding school in 1893. Even his two-year stay would have given him more access to education than many another farmer's son in villages like Tresham. Gran suggested that he was a shy boy and his mother intended this experience to "bring him out". But she also said on occasion that she found his reserved nature attractive – "romantic" – and like many of the descriptions she applied to her husband, the shyness was equally a feature of her son. Was their education intended to make them bolder, more confident? Or was it a rite of passage, an initiation?

But one motivation should not be lightly ignored. Grandfather went to school in an age with a strong focus on "improvement". This did not necessarily mean that Robert Thomas was going to learn the sort of arithmetic which would help him in buying and selling cattle. It did mean acquiring a veneer of schooled behaviour that might attract a more socially advanced set of friends – and even a wife whose own background might speak of social advancement. Robert Thomas's parents did not, in making this decision, break with the rooted non-conformity of the Cotswold valleys, for they sent their son to a Methodist school. The educational choices, whatever else they indicate, suggest something of the social aspirations of a family, now in a settled way of life halfway up the valley at Tresham, who saw themselves moving confidently forward, onto the escarpment itself, making better marriage alliances.

Robert Thomas is listed as having attended "Form IV" but beyond that we know little other than at age 16 he was back on the farm at Tresham. We gather that he was 20 when he caught the flashing eyes of the eldest of the Hatherall girls. The youngest of those girls, Lillian (Auntie Lil) described him as quiet and well-spoken. Would he have wanted his son to follow him to Wycliffe? None of them could have known the dreadful backdrop to that decision. The death of Robert Thomas before the age of 40 not only shook the economic foundations of the family at Tresham, but it asked questions about the running of the household. We are talking about a time when labour was cheap and plentiful. We have seen that Robert Thomas had entanglements with the indoor help, but Gran expected, as a farmer's wife would have done, adequate levels of support in nursery and kitchen. When that was not forthcoming after her husband's death, other measures had to be taken.

Father always noted the amount of time he spent away from

home after that untimely event. Staff reductions were necessary. The eldest boy spent a lot of time with his grandmother and great-aunt, and they taught him a great deal. Perhaps he got less from prolonged stays with his Clark cousins – the cold and the religiosity were his abiding memories. Riding Billy to the Dame school in Tetbury left a mark on him, but perhaps not for what he learned in the classroom. He left behind frantic activity, whether at Tresham or subsequently at Calcot, since Gran was now a farmer and cattle dealer, a partner with delinquent brothers, and a housewife with four children.

There was little time for Father. As the farming enterprises slid into economic collapse in recession and Gran's need for emotional support drove her towards men who could provide it, her children were delegated to others. Her eldest, aged ten in 1918, was probably as confused as I was at the same age in 1955: the eldest son, the expectation of succession, the lack of a role model.

He spoke of these years with a degree of bitterness, a feeling of having been pushed away. Although his admiration for his mother's energy and resolve in these hard years never diminished, and he never ceased to love her and obey her, she created a strongly matriarchal family unit in which judgement was swift and final, and also at times draconian and unjust. When it was decided that Father should go to Wycliffe, three years after his father's death, the decision could have been a relief, just as the death had been in the first instance. The decision had financial support from his grandparents.

He describes his early months at school in terms of desperate homesickness, especially for his brothers and for Billy the pony. But Matron was kind to him and gave him a sweet – a sugar cube pressed into a hole in an orange which you sucked – when he was unable to sleep.

During his life I was able to see him with three of his school friends and hear their reminiscences. All recalled his horticultural abilities. F. Mark Kenchington remembered his bargaining with other boys to take over their ten feet by ten feet garden plots – every boy had a garden to tend and they were regularly inspected to ensure that they were not neglected. Henry "Tiger" Rivers recalled Father as an entrepreneur, growing vegetables on these plots to supply fresh produce to the wives of teachers. S. H. G. Looseley was another friend who returned to the school to teach after graduating in mathematics from St John's College, Cambridge. By the time I reached Wycliffe he had become headmaster.

"And, do you know, David, by the time of your Father leaving the school, his vegetables were so important to the wives that they got up a petition asking him to stay on."

Asking Father about these early signs of an entrepreneurial bent produced a half smile: "Well, they sent me away to school, but they all forgot that to survive I would need some pocket money."

Father was proud to be awarded the Batchelor Cup for gardening, but was unable to show us the trophy because it was lost in one of his mother's house moves.

Two teachers made a firm impression on Father. One was Tommy Reade, who Father remembered cycling round and round the school grounds shirtless in all elements and reading a copy of *The Times* attached to his handlebars. He taught Father maths. He was in semi-retirement by the time I arrived and I asked if he recalled my father.

"No," he responded testily, he could not be expected to recall every farm boy who had failed to learn arithmetic from him, and he was certain that he had never taught anyone with such an outlandish name as "Worlock"!

The other teacher was much more responsive. E. J. Bevan still taught Greek and Latin in the sixth form to the two or three classics students that Wycliffe produced every year. He taught the languages only: the literature was "pagan". He was tall, stood ramrod straight, and his emotionless, aquiline features recalled nineteenth-century photographs of Sitting Bull. The only time those features were animated was while preaching. This he did regularly as a lay preacher in the school chapel. I came to know that he also preached in an ancient, rusting "tin tabernacle" which sat in a tiny plot of land at the edge of the school grounds. Over the door it proclaimed itself the First Church of Bethel. Two of us boys asked E.J.B. if we could attend a service. He said we would be welcome, and so we sat at the back while members of the church prophesied and spoke in tongues. It was a religious experience like no other, and the leader in denunciation of the wicked and identification of their precise place in purgatory was our own reserved and withdrawn Latin master. His careful definitions of the role of the gerund, or the function of the ablative, never quite seemed the same subsequently.

E.J.B. remembered Father. The vegetables, of course, and "a very quiet boy, who left us before he could learn very much."

Indeed, that would be a conclusion that Father himself might have endorsed. He always spoke of himself as not being fully, or "properly" educated. Sometimes this was a blind, used to hoodwink someone who, whether he had decided or not, was about to buy a horse from Father.

"You wouldn't take advantage of a poor old man, like me, who never had your educational advantages and has only ever had one decent hoss in his life!"

These shameful acting performances left his family deeply embarrassed, but could be very affecting for the victims. Once, at Heath End Farm, a young merchant banker who aspired to look good with the Heythrop on Saturdays, brought his fiancée to witness the purchase of his mount. They got the full ignorant-farmer routine in a dealing session that concluded with the young woman tearfully begging her husband-to-be to return to and accept dear Mr Worlock's opening offer, because:

"John, you have the money and it would break my heart to take advantage of Mr Worlock in any way."

The wish for more education was always there, however, and I first encountered it walking up a red field at Broadclyst in Devon, with Bob Brownsey, the rough-hewn Keynsham butcher who had been Father's surprising choice as best man. Father and Bob were talking about keeping diaries, and I asked if either of them had read *Rural Rides*, which I was studying at school. It turned out that Bob was a dedicated Cobbett enthusiast, and our animated conversation took us to the top of the field.

"That's what I wish my education had given me, the ability to talk like that about things like that," said Father.

As we shall see, Father had a great deal of literature on board and was by no means uneducated in any sense. He did feel, however, that he might have come away from Wycliffe with more. A passionate reader in the second half of his life, he blamed his own inattention at school for what he had missed. He clearly thought, or had been told, that he was a difficult subject for education. Did his parents tell him this? He said that he was awkward as a child – "'ockerd" in the language of the lanes. Not someone to be shaped by education. And did the school contribute to this, with a view of a farmer's educational needs that did not run past the basics? If so, then I can testify that the prejudice was still there thirty years later.

Education Fit for Purpose

I ARRIVED AT Wycliffe happy, but confused. In the first place, my previous experiences of education had been a complete disaster. When I was five I went to Miss Lemon's school in Chipping Sodbury High Street, and the following year to a new school she founded in the same street. In the year after that I went to Yate C of E Primary School. Then the year after that I went to the Ridge Primary School on a new estate between Yate and Sodbury, and then the year after that to Mrs Shipp's school in the High Street again. Here, at the age of ten, with five different educational experiences behind me, I failed the eleven-plus examination.

What did Father think about all of this? First of all, he

distanced himself from it. In his view, education was a domestic issue. My mother should manage all these things. He had the farm. I was plainly ineducable, and he told me, in those fits of cursing that marked these years, that I had to be a farmer because I could not do anything else – but what sort of farmer would I be if, as it appeared, I could not learn or remember or recall a single thing? My mother clung to the idea that I was a "late developer", anxiously changing her mind every year on the basis of anecdotal evidence from friends and neighbours, and moved me on to a "better" school. So here lay confusion: in my heart I knew I could never be a farmer, yet here I was being educated to be one. And in public, especially with farming friends and relatives, the official line, delivered by both my parents and myself, was that I would, at school-leaving age, return home to be a farmer.

Then, in my first term at Wycliffe, this started to change. One day, a conscientious French teacher, Mr King, came and stood behind me as I copied down the homework he had just set from the blackboard. After a few moments of looking at the board and then my exercise book, he said,

"Worlock, why aren't you writing what I wrote?" And then he said, "Worlock, you cannot read the blackboard, can you?"

So five years of thinking I could see what everyone else saw, or pretending when I couldn't, dissolved away. After this I was soon a very short-sighted boy with spectacles, but in ability terms little different from my classmates.

And I was happy. No one wanted me to herd cattle or told me I was a failure, and, more particularly, I was not subject to moral blackmail.

"It costs an awful lot to go to Wycliffe – it really would be wise to go out and work alongside your father and show him that it will all be worth it."

I knew the deepening ravine in understanding between Father and myself was hurtful to my mother, and I sensed that they had probably reached deadlock on the subject. He would do no more to make a farming life seem congenial to me – indeed, part of his message was that such a life could not be congenial to anyone – you just had to "grin and bear it", as we said, so that you could get through to other things you liked more, like hunting. My mother, stretched between the two of us, was thus limited to being able to influence matters through her ability to influence me. She told me that it was really important for my future that, whatever I had determined in my own mind, and which I might "grow out of", that I try to keep Father hopeful that I might succeed him. Anything I could do at Wycliffe that would help him to hold on to that hope would help me. I took her words, as always, very seriously.

As it happened, Wycliffe first encountered and characterised me as the very person I did not want to be – the farmer's son. This was not so obvious in the junior school but once I had moved into Haywardsfield, I became a stock figure of agricultural type-casting. The school had a small pig farm, wedged into five acres of wasteland between the main road at the foot of the school grounds and a single-track railway line used to bring timber to the adjacent Ryeford Saw Mills. It had eight breeding sows, and some seventy weaners being brought forward for bacon, and a contract to supply a nearby bacon factory.

The school Young Farmers Club had some twenty-five members who shared on rota the farmwork involved, to be conducted before and after school each day. I met the woodwork teacher, P. J. "Crow" Parrott, who immediately enrolled me and set me to work on the swill-collection duty, fetching kitchen waste from the school dining rooms to boil up in our ancient boiler to feed to growing baconers. Then I reported back to my mother, who in turn responded that this was just what she had in mind. Keeping the idea alive that I might return to the farm would be vital if I was to be allowed to stay at school after the official school-leaving age. That age was then 15.

So now I began to live a two-track life. One was for home consumption, dedicated to inculcating the idea that I was still a committed agriculturalist, finding my way back to the cowshed by a different route, but still loyal to the succession plan. The other was the development of the ten-year-old would-be autodidact into a passionate student of history and English literature, who responded to the inspiration of three wonderful teachers and began to grow intellectual aspirations. As firmly as I knew that I would never be a farmer, so firmly did I know that I wanted to study history for as long as anyone would allow me to do so. But even at the age of 14 I could see that my two tracks diverged at a future point. The man with the flags who would signal the parting of the ways was the headmaster – and Father's old friend from his own school days – Stanley George Henry Looseley.

My contemporaries at school have always assured me that the headmaster was a "good man". My experience was that he was a man of rock-hard assumptions, like the careers teacher who missed me off the schedule of career-choice interviews because he "knew" that I already had a career in farming. The headmaster called me in to talk about O Level choices, then the school-leaving qualification later displaced by GCSEs. He did not beat about the bush, pointing out that neither French nor Latin would serve me well in the Rickyard, so he had removed those subjects from my burdens and replaced them with woodwork and art:

"I expect even farmers find a moment to go to an art gallery."

This, he said, would be less burdensome, but he did not have high expectations of me. I was to do as well as I could, and since he had removed any sciences, general or specific, I would find I had some free periods which would help, he was sure, with Young Farmers' activities. I left his study in a daze, though in retrospect his air of contentment may have betrayed the satisfaction of a man who had just solved some difficult setting and timetabling issues. He did not communicate his decisions to my parents.

And in truth I did not protest. The subject I hated was maths, taught by Crow Parrott either in class, or in his woodwork class, or as I sat on the wall of his piggery at Slad near Stroud, watching his boar serve the gilts that I had helped him bring up from the school. Though I would never be a farmer, I did love pigs, for their gregariousness, their curiosity, and their philosophical sagacity. Some of the older sows on the school farm heard my troubles and disappointments so many times that they would go and lie down when I started speaking to them. So when, in that year, as I was bringing my swill trolley down the school drive to cross the road to the farm, I heard a train whistle, urgent and repeated, I abandoned the swill and ran across the level crossing. The driver of the little train that brought the timber was leaning out of his cab.

"Your piggery is on fire," he yelled as I ran past.

First things first. I unlocked the door and climbed into our little office. It was full of smoke, but the phone was still working. I called 999. That done, the first thing was to release pigs. I had been in a farm fire before. The front part of the building was clearly ablaze – the fire brigade said the oil feed on our ancient boiler had become detached, the oil had run into the guttering on either side of the pigsties and flames had leapt up the walls igniting the straw we suspended above the pigs for insulation. So the pigs had to be released from the other end of the building. By this time other boys were arriving. We opened the nearest sties and and once the sty gates were open, hysterical pigs burst out, eyes rolling in fear. But not in numbers enough.

Several of us wetted our handkerchiefs in the water butt, put them over nose and mouth and crawled up the cleaning corridor that connected the sties. More pigs came away, then a pen of strangely stunned animals who only moved when pushed and shoved. Then a pen of pig statues, and as I struck one on the backside, I felt it was melting. Beyond that pen we could not go as the heat and smoke and cascades of burning straw made it too dangerous. The fire brigade quickly got things under control and soon we were crawling back in with Crow and the vet with humane killers. We lost twenty-three bacon pigs.

If I thought this event would catch Father's attention, I was quite wrong. It was almost as if going away to school had put me in an isolation ward. We now never spoke about farming. In fact we scarcely ever spoke at all. This saddened my mother and her sadness depressed me. She thought that his unwillingness to engage with me signalled that he was awaiting some move on my part which would allow him to recognise me as his farmer successor.

"It's up to you," she would tell me, intimating that getting this right was the hinge upon which studying any more history after O levels swung.

And so developed a plan, at first by chance and then more confidently and deftly as the year went on. It rested on two things close to Father's heart. The first was the heritage around the farms and the Cotswold way of life, including hunting. The other was "judging the animal", a skill which Father considered that he had mastered to a high degree. The fact that I had just been elected Secretary of the Young Farmers, and would be their President the following year, put instruments into my hands. I had to create an agenda for club events for the coming year, and I was in charge of entering Young Farmers into county and national competitions.

My first move on the agenda front was to arrange a farm walk. Traditionally a farmer with a good story to tell (successful rotations, effective use of fertiliser, mechanisation, control of labour costs) would take the club members round the farm and talk about their methods. So, via my mother, I enquired whether Father would undertake this for his old school. My mother said she would provide a tea for everyone. But the answer was a refusal – was I trying to show him up? was the question.

So I then got in touch with a local farmer at Horsley, Bertram Cox. He was the friend of Uncle Dick's who had travelled to Australia with him. His son, John, had been at Wycliffe a year ahead of me but had left as soon as he could to get back on the farm. Given this encouraging background, would Father join us on the walk and provide his own views as we went along? Bertram said yes, his wife Mary produced a cream tea that lives in the memory sixty years later, but Father declined to come at the last minute.

During the Autumn and Spring terms we tried to hold weekly evening meetings. Some of these were devoted to discussing our pigs. Others were filled with travel films and anything we could get free from suppliers. But I was determined we should have star speakers of the sort that Father would recognise as his peers, and that he should be invited to the meetings. Other farmer fathers came along and often asked good questions that helped us understand.

So on 30 November 1962 I introduced Jim King, of Calcot Farm Nailsworth (now the Calcot Manor Hotel), a man who

Father had often described as the best farmer in the Cotswolds, and who had led a renaissance in that farm's fortunes after its pre-war disasters. Given his intimate knowledge of that farm – it was after all the place where Father was born – I thought Father could not resist.

And then, in the spring, I rolled out this agenda:

1 Feb	Lt Col Frank Weldon, former British Olympic Equestrian team captain (*Father: "the finest rider of my generation"*)	
15 Feb	Mr E. M. Mitchell, Manager of the Beaufort Estates	
15 March	Major R. Dallas, Secretary of the Beaufort Hunt	
22 March	Mr Jack Windell, The Home Farm, Badminton (*Father's oldest hunting friend*)	

I passed back the message that these were the people he said you could learn from, about farming and the Cotswold heritage. My mother was lavish in her praise, but of course I had only got these people to attend by using my father's name. I wanted to show him I had listened to and heard what he had said. He was invited to join us, and many of the speakers anticipated seeing him there in their letters. They were to be disappointed. He never came to listen to any of them.

I had tried really hard to impress him, and I had failed. My best guess was that, in line with the eleven-plus exam, he meant exactly what he had said about my failure. In his terms it wasn't that I couldn't be a farmer because I did not want to be one. He had written me off because I lacked the intellectual and physical capacity to do the job and, again like the eleven-plus, it was a final judgement which could not be amended over time. I had been judged, found wanting, and therefore discussing it simply wasted more time and energy. Yet my mother could not bear the thought of what she described as a "breach" between father and son. I certainly did not want to be dragged away from school just when I was finding out what school might offer me.

One last effort was called for, and the instrument was to hand. Some time earlier I had entered the Young Farmers into the County Young Farmers' pig-judging competition, but we were too young to enter as individuals, so we took part as a team. We learnt a lot judging a pen of four bacon pigs, we enjoyed being in the Gloucester market on our own, and we were pleased that we came third, since we had little experience. We came home and practised, using our own pigs and estimating deadweights which we later checked with C & T Harris (Calne) Ltd, who took our pigs for slaughter.

Soon May came round again and I could enter the competition individually, but still only as an "intermediate" in the below-18 age group. After my turn was over I listened to the rest of the intermediate class and then the seniors as they presented to the panel of judges. Did I sound like that, I wondered? While their reasoning was usually excellent, their presentation certainly wasn't. In my other life at school I had become a keen debater. That year I had gone to the extempore speaking competition at the Cheltenham Festival. I held the glorious rank of Serjeant-At-Arms in the Wycliffe College Literary and Debating Society ("LitSoc"). I was no longer a tongue-tied farmer's son: I could speak. I knew that it could be a real weapon. While my pig knowledge was as good as but not better than the next young farmer, I should be able to paint a picture for the judges that touched their imaginations and which was memorable when it came to scoring.

So we came to 17 May 1963. At last I was in the senior competition, which had entrants up to the age of 30. They looked very old to me. I was the only entrant from a school-based club. I had briefed my mother carefully and told her the café I would go to between the judging rounds. I judged two pens of pigs in the morning and was still in contention after the elimination round. I felt so sure Father would come: the prizes were being presented by the President of the Gloucestershire Young Farmers' Federation, His Grace the Duke of Beaufort. Himself!

I had still not seen them when the last round began. Parents of school friends who were worried that I had not eaten passed me a pork pie, and the irony of nibbling it while peering over the railings for the first sight of the last pen of pigs, the results of which would decide the winner, caused me wry amusement.

Four fine bacon pigs. Four flop-eared Wessex Saddlebacks, not a fashionable pig in the age of Danish Landrace. The judges were keen on traditional breeds: we always had a pen of Large Whites and often one of Gloucester Old Spots. The game was to judge each pig in terms of its value and likely productivity as a meat producer, and the panel judging the contestants did so on the basis of the arguments used to differentiate each of the pigs from the others as we placed them in order of merit. Each contestant had ten minutes to outline his reasoning. When I began this seemed an eternity. By this final year I was worried about getting my reasoning into the time, leaving me no chance to search the crowd of faces around the ring for the face of Father.

At last it was my turn. Having a name beginning with " W" can be burdensome in an alphabetical world. Here it carried an advantage. The panel had heard us all several times already that day. The litany of issues raised was limited in scope. The panel had heard the same issues described in the same way and were getting bored. They sat in one of the sale rings, at best a noisy place, and the reserved and nervous Young Farmers spoke softly and tentatively. It was not hard therefore to speak in a louder voice and project it round the ring. One of the pigs had an eye infection that had closed one eye while another had a slight limp, so I announced that I was not going to mark down these two pigs, so obviously named Horatio and Hopalong, for factors that did not impact on their bacon qualities. In the context of the day this counted as wild, knockabout humour and I grew in confidence when I saw some of the panel smile, and all of them sit back from their notes and look at me directly.

My ten minutes were soon done. Then there was the wait for the scoring. The crowd had thinned and it was clear it contained no Father. The announcement that I had won, the flaccid ducal handshake from a bored aristocrat who said not a word, the cup (retained by the school) and the certificate presentation were all events that went by me in moments. Only the parting words of the organizing secretary remained in my head as I boarded the little train back to Stonehouse.

"Of course, you realise you will have an automatic place to represent Gloucestershire in the national competition in Smithfield in the autumn. See you there ..."

No, you really won't, I thought. *Pig judging is now done, and so is impressing people who will not be impressed, and so is trying to persuade anyone that I will ever be a farmer. Let the truth be out: I have not a clue what to do except that it will never be farming.*

Chapter 18

Plots and Indecisions

ERE WE NEED to make a declaration. The dramatic action at this point seems to demand heroes and villains. Praise and blame should be ladled out and attached to the participants according to merit. Someone should be arraigned in the dock of history and retrospective sentences should be handed out. Yet over fifty years have elapsed, and the one conclusion that can be drawn by me about these events is the striking muddle of mixed motives that afflicted all of the participants. In particular, my mother was protecting her husband and her son, and her relationship with each of them. The headmaster was doing what he thought was best for his old school friend and, a precious feature, his relationship with university admissions tutors in those days before a unified university entrance system.

Father and I had much in common: unreasonable stubbornness, "the Sin of Pride", and that quality which Gran described when she said her son was quite unable to "do anything in a way that any normal person would do it." Father called this his "'ockerdness", and like these other qualities I had it in full. Like Uncle Critch Pope at the wheel of the Bristol racer we were each driving as fast as we could towards the Westonbirt crossroads. It would take a miracle not to crash – and another if we both recovered from such a crash. The first miracle was not to be forthcoming.

O Levels were not to be my moment of triumph. I passed well in history and English and geography. I just got woodwork (30% on the practical work, but 75% on the history of furniture in the eighteenth century). Art went the other way, though I got a distinction on a paper on the art and architecture of the English Parish Church, which delivered a lifetime of joy and satisfaction since it gave me the wherewithal to "read" and date the gothic styles. Alas, no maths. Failed to be a farmer, failed eleven-plus, failed his O Levels. What did I want to fail at next?

The answer, to me at least, was obvious. If I was to satisfy my new ambition to go to university and study history, then I needed three good passes at Advanced (A) Level. My subjects were obviously to be the three in which I already had good passes at O level. And having given up trying to impress Father through Young Farmers I had branched out into other things, which were helping me to establish myself as a "character" in the life of the school. As my views on the immorality of centre-right politics, the pointlessness of monarchy or the hypocrisy of organised religion took on the shrill edge of teenage dissonance, so I expressed them ever more insistently and rumbustiously as

I rose to become Secretary and then President of the Literary and Debating Society. The master in charge of the Society, who attended every debate, was the new chaplain, ex-RAF, an Irish Protestant from the South. He recognised me as someone who did not quite fit, and for reasons I will never quite resolve satisfactorily in my own mind, he decided to make me notorious.

Every time, it seemed to me, that I spoke in debates, my adolescent views were amplified from the pulpit at morning prayers or shot down in the Sunday sermon.

"On Thursday night in the LitSoc," thundered the sonorous tones of West Cork, "the Communist member for Chipping Sodbury, like Samson Agonistes, tore at the fabric of Church and State ..."

"The other evening in the LitSoc, the leader of our Marxist minority, before spraying us all with machine-gun bullets to make us better people, opined that ..."

And so I became known, and took on over the next few years many other roles in the life of the school, whose story belongs elsewhere. But the chaplain spoke to me about my ambitions, and I made them known to my history teachers, and to the very wonderful head of English who was my deputy housemaster. All promised, in the language of influence, to "put in a word" and indicated that they wanted me to go on. My parents, meanwhile, had received the final term bill and a letter from the bursar that said that I was not expected back at the end of the summer. Just when life was opening up, my options seemed to be closing down.

And then they opened up again. Father received a letter from his old friend the headmaster. It invited him and my mother to lunch at the end of term, and I could join them afterwards for a discussion. He understood from colleagues that I had desires to stay on and he wanted to confirm that leaving was the decision and the family consensus. As soon as my mother told me the news I saw it as a lifeline. I made it clear to her how desperate I was to stay. If I was to do anything non-agricultural in life I must get some qualifications. Or could she imagine the war zone created by Father and me trying to work on the same farm?

She promised to do her best, but felt that the money was going to be the key issue, and, anyway, wouldn't it have been wasted if I did not get to a university? Father, she said, kept saying that no Worlock had ever been to a university and he did not see why that should ever alter.

By the time of the meeting I was in alternating mode, winning the argument in my own mind and then losing it under a withering fire of headmasterly questions. As morning school ended I saw that Father's car was parked outside of the headmaster's house at the bottom of the school grounds. At 2.30 p.m. I knocked on the headmaster's door and was shown into the dining room.

"Come in, David," said the Head cheerily. "Robert and I have had a very good discussion about your future and made what I think are some very sound decisions. Sit down and we will tell you all about it!"

I took in the room. The headmaster at the head of the table. His wife now clearing away some plates. Father, with the deep flush that a few glasses of wine always induced … and my mother was not there. What could they possibly have decided without any input from anyone who understood what I might want? But then, what he might want had never been an issue in deciding what happened in Father's life, so why should it figure in mine?

Smiling reassuringly at Father, the Head, in his role of chair-man of the board, began to sum up the meeting.

"David, your father needs you. You have a clear responsibility to your parents to take on the farm. Your sisters will get married and leave, no doubt, but your father cannot go on farming for ever. He will want to retire, but he has every right to expect that you will continue the enterprise in a way that supports him and your mother in their old age, and we all hope that you too will marry in due course and provide a further succession. Why, I have seen hundreds of farmers' sons go through this school, and this was always the pattern and ever will be. Some things change, eh, Robert? But not farmers or farming!

"We also talked, David, about the representations made to me by the chaplain and your history and English teachers. You have given them to understand that you nurse an ambition to attend university. That is patently absurd. You are not the stuff of which scholars are made, and I fail to see how it would make you a better farmer, and in any case your qualifications, or lack of them, would prohibit it. You would need three good A level grades. Plus maths at O level, which you failed. Plus Latin, which you gave up after a year of study four years ago, at the same level. This would be an impossible burden and I cannot imagine it can be done, but as I say, my sixth form specialists seem keen if we can find a way.

"Your mother has indicated that she will be agreeable to any solution that both your father and you yourself agree. The chaplain has said he will teach you Latin at night – apparently he is teaching his mother A level Latin at the same time. I can timetable you for retaking your maths. So there is a possibility that you can stay for one more year, but your father and I have agreed some strict conditions. If you fail your Latin or your maths then you will give up this foolishness and accept reality. And please do not expect me to put you forward for a university place. When I endorse a candidate to a university admissions tutor they accept my word. They know the school reputation. We simply cannot allow marginal candidates – or people, David, who are likely to drop out if the going gets hard, and return to the farm – to go through the system. Think how you would feel if you learnt that because you did not last the course, or got a poor degree, other candidates from Wycliffe were turned down and thus denied achieving their full potential.

"So talk to your parents and your teachers, David, and let me know by next week. I fear you have little chance of success, but I see we must demonstrate to you through your own failure the conclusion that your father and I have reached over lunch: that the only place for you in life is on the farm, and whatever else you learn, you must learn the importance of inuring yourself to that fact."

So Father was right after all? The most important lesson in life was learning how cheerfully to do those things that you least wanted to do? Move those bricks across the Little Tump – and then move them back again. Obey and do not question. Accept your fate, embrace your destiny.

Father turned to go, thanking the headmaster as he did so. Then, as he climbed into the car, he realised that he had not said farewell to his son. Half rising out of the drivers seat, he awkwardly extended his hand to me, and I, equally awkwardly, shook it. As he closed the door I walked past the car and up the path that led back to the school. With my back to what had passed, I began to smile, and then, as I passed the woodwork shop, to laugh aloud.

I had another year! Anything could happen in that impossibly long time. Who knows, I might pass all those exams.

My situation could change completely, but all through that year I would at least be reading and studying those things that interested me most. And it was another year when I could not be made to be a farmer, and something told me that the more years passed, the less likely it was that my hand could still be forced.

So I returned to Haywardsfield and sat down in the Common Room and started to do something I had been thinking about for weeks. I started to write a short narrative of the American Civil War. Reaching about ten thousand words and eventually typed by my mother, my history teachers sent it to an academic at Exeter University, C. P. Hill, whose comments gave me huge encouragement. I was 16. I was on my way. I knew I could write and study history, and I had one more year at Wycliffe to make it all come true.

The story of the next year and the year after belong in another context, since Father was the person least concerned with them. I did get the grades I needed in history, English and geography to get to university. I did pass maths. I failed three more attempts at Latin, despite spending my evenings at the chaplain's fireside and committing whole chunks of *De Bello Gallico* to memory.

All parties stuck to the agreement made at that meeting. The Head did not endorse me as a university candidate. I left school to learn Latin by night in London (and then got two passes), and eventually – with the support of the chaplain, the two history teachers and the evidence of my writing – I got interviewed by five universities, was awarded places at Sussex and Cambridge, and ended up at Selwyn College, Cambridge, for three years that changed my life completely.

Father was not much aware of this. In later years he once asked me how I got through that year in London financially, and was surprised when I said that I worked by day; but it could not have happened had my mother not paid for the Latin classes and rented my sister Mo's spare room for me, since neither my life as a Gallup pollster nor as a labourer laying cobblestones the length of Holland Park Mews would have paid the bills. And she would not have let me go had not Uncle Don, now promoted to Shell Head Office in the Strand (in a small room with a rug and one picture, but he assured me he would rise to three pictures and fitted carpets), regularly taken me to the Regent Palace Hotel carvery to feed me, and to check and report back.

Father said he knew he had written no cheques so it must have come out of the housekeeping. He said this as if he was aware of what the cheques were intended for that he was signing. He lived in a world of total trust in my mother's financial management. In later years she would hand him the chequebook and ask him to sign a dozen blanks for her if she had bills to pay.

His disengagement from my life was now complete. He had never, of course, been an engaged parent, and maybe this reflected his mother's attitudes to him. You would never expect to see him at the school play if you were performing, or at speech day if you got a prize. I recall overhearing Gran say of Joyce's enthusiasm for her daughter, Sue, and her riding career,

"You can overindulge children by taking an interest in them, by taking them everywhere and by clapping when they win – they end up thinking they are important."

If this was a danger then Father shielded us from it very effectively. He was simply not a part of the lives of his children unless their lives somehow intersected with his – usually on a hunting field. Otherwise, the lives of children were my mother's domain. She did the worrying and the support. She told me to persevere when I was depressed. She drove past the school when she thought my letters indicated need, and left a cake for my tuck box without "disturbing" me.

And she felt guilty about what had happened in what we afterwards referred to as "the meeting" or sometimes "the meeting that you never attended". I always suspected that Uncle Don gave her a hard time over it. He saw himself as a modern man in this regard, pointing to a world where at least half of the school-leaving population would need degrees. He felt that he and his brother were cheated of their chance, noted that his niece did biology at London and said his two children would be brought up to believe that a university education was their birthright.

"What is it with you Worlocks that makes you think that a university education is some sort of breakthrough?"

But Uncle Don had no knowledge of the succession syndrome in Cotswold farming communities.

Chapter 19

Of Uplands and Downlands

ATHER AND I NEVER SPOKE about "the meeting", nor through long years of companionable friendship that began when my university life was over did he ever mention the decisions that he and the Head thought they had reached. My mother was equally reserved on the subject. She never told me why she did not attend the meeting, and I never asked. I assumed that she felt that an argument might break out, and that she would be caught in the middle; her loyalties would be strained but her duty to her husband would prevail. She did not want to do that in front of me. "Duty" was a heavyweight word with crushing implications in my childhood. It usually meant that you were about to do something that you really did not want to do. Rather than obligations happily embraced as part of reciprocal relationships, duty usually entailed someone enforcing their will on someone weaker than themselves. In a world where feudal duties were still warm in the grave, familial duty was very much alive and kicking.

Yet it would be wrong to suggest that in the Cold War atmosphere surrounding what Gran and others described as my "future" ("What are you going to do about your future, Dave?") family life disappeared entirely. In fact, everything went on very normally. I concentrated on my studies, of which there were many. In school holidays I concentrated even harder. My mother ceased to tell me that I really should be helping my father, and he almost ceased noticing that I was there at all. That first year after the meeting, with the "decision" made, gave everyone the comfort that something had been done, matters had been resolved.

Thus, wonderfully, great pressure was lifted from me – all I had to do was to pass five examinations. Great pressure was also released from Father. Whether or not he ever believed that failure would drive me back to the morning and evening attachment to milking cows, his position was now clear and in his mind I was bound to the agreement he had reached with the Head.

So we had no need to argue further – or even discuss it. My mother certainly did not want it mentioned. So it wasn't, and the fact that it wasn't led to one of the most extraordinary long weekends of my young life. It came about because Father, planning his move away from the Beaufort Hunt and into the fast-paced world of the Heythrop in the North Cotswolds, had met the charismatic Ronnie Wallace while the latter was having a day's sport as a guest of the Duke. Ronnie had warmed to the hunting farmer who said he longed to buy a farm in Heythrop country, and felt he should be encouraged. He invited Father to have a couple of days on Exmoor with him at the end of the hunting season and enjoy the stag hunting there. Wallace himself had an interest in the Devon and Somerset staghounds (to which he retired once his Heythrop days were done).

For several reasons this invitation prompted a domestic crisis at Nibley Farm. In the first instance Father was determined to go. No argument of logistics would deter him. Yes, he knew he would need two horses. Yes, he knew he would need a livery stable and a groom to bring him the second horse when the first got exhausted. Yes, he knew it was very different country from the Cotswolds. Yes, he realised all of this would be expensive. Yes, the milking was a problem but he was sure that Ben, with the help of Jane's husband, Frank Weekes, could cope for a few days. In short it was clear he just had to go, which created a real problem for my mother. Both Jane and Mary were married with young families, and she had made childcare commitments that she could not, and did not, want to renege upon. As she explained to me, normally she would have asked my sister Mo, closest to him in terms of horses and hunting, to go with him, but Mo was now a teacher in a London comprehensive school and could not simply be called to perform. Which was why, my mother said, she was asking me to be his minder.

This was wholly different from all those pleas to go and work alongside Father and be a farmer's son. She began by describing all of the risks to which he would be exposed if, as he now indicated, he went alone because no one would go with him. First of all, he would lose his way without a navigator. Then he would fall asleep at the wheel: it was ninety miles and his normal journey was about five. Then again he would need to stop, refuel and have a tea or coffee: how was this possible unless someone told him where to stop and had the money ready to settle the bills? And, she said, she knew I was aware of his habit of driving at high speed through boring towns and then dawdling through farmland so he could criticise the farming efforts of others. What if the police stopped him, or he had a puncture? Who would safely carry the driver's licence and insurance certificate and have them ready at the right time? The answer, apparently, to all of these questions was a 17-year-old boy, not his 54-year-old parent!

In this request I suddenly learnt very many things which had previously been obscure to me. It was a shock to think that my mother thought I was more adult and responsible than Father. It was the first instance – there were to be many later on, in particular involving the sale of land – where I became the interface with the real world (and people like lawyers or accountants or surveyors or land agents, who all bored him) while he concentrated on the important matters, like the hunting. I suspect that the process by which first his mother, and then mine, made him dependent and then turned him back into a child was one, as an acutely intelligent person, he was happy to accept. Being robbed of responsibility was being robbed of worry, and he must have welcomed that. Farming had worries enough from the haphazard strikes of disease, adverse weather or impaired cash flow. The trip to Exmoor was my first recognition of my mother's belief that I would grow up as a person at once capable and responsible, like her dear brothers. But not like Father. Her confidence in me made me accept a trip that I would normally have refused categorically.

Whatever the subsequent thoughts and rationalisations, the long weekend itself was perfectly and consistently bizarre. It was four days spent with Tristram Shandy's Uncle Toby. In the first instance we had the difficulty of reaching our destination, the Anchor Hotel at Porlock Weir, because Father was convinced that the Land Rover would expire in its own boiling oil if he attempted to drive it up Porlock Hill, a notorious 1:4 incline with acute bends, sanded escape roads, said to be the steepest A road in Britain. I looked it up on the map. The hill is actually to the west of Porlock, which meant that coming from Minehead on the A39 we would reach the hotel before the hill. My driver was not convinced. In fact he looked like a horse that, having refused a fence, is fairly determined not to have another go. Heavy, snickering nose blowing and rolling eyes, showing the whites. We stopped in Minehead and sat in a café to sort things out. I showed him the maps. He remained unconvinced. He had never read a map, so while he thought things through I went into the second-hand bookshop next door to the café.

There I found what I was looking for almost immediately. A book as thick as a loaf of bread. A book I could climb into for the weekend, pulling the covers down over my head for protection. *The Life of Arthur, Duke of Wellington* by Rev G. R. Gleig. The 1862 Longman edition, leather-bound in burgundy. Gleig was a young infantryman at the end of the Peninsular War, and in a life in the military (he was Army chaplain and Inspector of Army Schools when he wrote this book many years later) he knew both the Duke and many of his generals. I could have sat down with it then and there, but a choice had been made next door. A brilliant idea emerged: we would drive to Exford, in the middle of Exmoor where the Hunt kennels were, and ask for guidance. This we did, arriving mid-afternoon.

The kennels were full of advice:

"Why didn't you go straight from Minehead – it was only a few miles."

"Porlock Hill comes after the village – now you are beyond it you will have to go down the hill to get to the hotel."

We got back into the Land Rover in silence. I started to turn the pages, knowing that Rev Gleig would be better company.

When we got to the top of the hill we thought again. We drew into a lay-by and discussed brakes for a little while. Father was confident. We had bought two Land Rovers, formerly the property of the Kenya National Parks Service. Some contractual obligation had meant that they had to be returned from the colonies to be sold, and we bought two on the clever theory that we could cannibalise one to keep the other on the road. This we had been doing, but Father had a certainty that he had been told that one of them had brakes which were only just adequate. But which one?

As we debated this interesting point, and agreed that going down the hill might be far more dangerous than going up, an AA patrolman on the then traditional motorbike and sidecar drew in beside us. Father scented salvation. He hurried over and explained the dilemma, ending with a request for help to test the brakes to see if they could survive the hill, with a Rice trailer and two restless horses on behind.

"Are you a member, sir?" asked the patrolman with a slightly suspicious tone.

"Of course," lied Father. "Indeed I was an early member, advised to join by my father-in-law, a senior policeman in Gloucestershire, where we come from."

"Oh, yes," said the patrolman. "You have no AA badge on the vehicle but I expect you have the certificate about you and are able to show it to me."

Father turned to me immediately. "Do we have the certificate amongst the paperwork your mother entrusted to you?"

When I demurred, he excused me as a mere boy who could not be expected to remember everything.

"His grandfather said we should always carry it in case someone like you asked. No one listens these days."

The patrolman tried another tack.

"Well, I was a policeman in Gloucestershire for twenty years – before I was early retired. Who was this grandfather of his?"

"Detective Inspector Simons."

"Inspector Sam? I loved that man. One of my heroes ..."

And in no time we were taking the trailer off, walking the horses, testing the brakes and, a divine mercy, plugging the trailer lights and brakes – and brake lights – into the Land Rover's systems for the first time that day. We then drove as slowly as we could to the bottom of the hill, with a motorcycle outrider, who gave us a cheery salute as he rode away at the bottom.

There were two hotels in Porlock Weir. The Porlock Weir was quite grand, and a favourite of my parents in later years. We stayed at the Anchor because it was the one with the livery stable. They both faced the little dock and the sheds that had once handled a fish catch. It was pre-holiday season in an age when tourism was not yet the staple industry of the West Country. The hotel seemed a little sad and damp to me, and the clerk at the desk was taking no prisoners.

"Have you reserved?" he said. "If not, I shall have to check availability."

"We booked the stables," began Father defensively.

"Different enterprise," interrupted the clerk. "See Red and George for that." The way he said it they sounded like one person – Red'n George. "Did you book rooms?"

Father now adopted the exasperated tone of one who cannot get the right quality of servants, as he turned to me.

"Well, did we? Don't dissemble, just tell the man the truth."

So I did. As the young clerk searched for rooms Father moved into the unctuous act he usually adopted to waiters and all others in service roles with whom he saw he needed to ingratiate himself.

"Well, Anthony (he called them all Anthony), I see you are a powerful chap in these parts. Lot of responsibility running a big hotel like this. I bet you can easily find us what we need."

"Depends what you want, for a start," said Anthony. (Actually, his name was Sean, and Birmingham Irish and less than a week into his first job since leaving school, I subsequently discovered.) "Superior or de Luxe?"

Father had never booked an hotel room in his life, he confessed over dinner. But, he claimed, he had erred on the side of caution since he did not know how much money my mother had furnished me with for the trip and thirty shillings a night had sounded expensive to him, so we only had one room, with a very solid-looking bolster to lay down the middle of a large double bed. The priority, he pointed out, was the horses, so we unboxed them and led them round to the livery area.

There we found two ancients, both in their early seventies, and both former hunt servants of the Devon and Somerset. They fell upon our animals with delight, rubbing them down with rolls of straw and feeding them a warm mash. The horses looked startled, as if without saying anything, they had suddenly moved from less than Superior into de Luxe. Their hosts, Red and George, were knowledgeable and loquacious.

"You brought these here to sell 'em?" asked George, immediately plumbing the depths of Father's ambitions as soon as he saw him.

"Bit big for moor country," said Red, adroitly summing up the findings of the following two days before they happened.

It was arranged that Red, whose shock of white hair had once been that colour, would ride second horse and act as guide. The first meet, on Saturday, was at Culbone and the second, on Monday, on Dunkery. Each very hackable, so I could see nothing to distract me from the Rev G. R. Gleig.

The sound of waves lapping on the inlet shores was a new and very pleasant experience for me as I lay in bed that first night. Soon it was replaced by Father's stentorian snoring, as if a dozen ocean-going tugs were clamouring to enter the tiny harbour all at once.

And then the actions began. First, rhythmic movement of hands and knees while lying on his front. Then, getting faster and faster until, as a climax, he seemed to become airborne, then lying prone on his back snoring until he turned over and it all began again.

My poor mother, I thought, and that first night I took a pillow, a blanket and Rev Gleig and climbed into the bath. Later, hearing odd, strangled words emerging from the sleeper (I caught "up", "quick" and "whoa" on several occasions, I realised that this was a jumping sequence). In his sleep, he was cantering across a field, and then, the target post and rails having been identified, he moved to a gallop to get the impulsion to jump it. There followed take-off and landing with perfect logic. Was the sleeper aware of the satisfaction of successful jumps? Did he ever fall off/out of bed? Did this betray underlying nervousness about the dangers of hunting, or the rush of adrenalin that drove him forward?

The next morning Father rode off early with Red while I climbed back into bed for some restorative sleep. Then a late breakfast with Rev Gleig while inspecting the defences of Ciudad Rodrigo under the cold eye of the impassive duke. Next a ramble around the breakwaters and harbour of the tiny fishing village, then back to the Anchor for a pint of IPA served by Anthony, aka Sean – two underage drinkers free from adult regulation. Then sitting on an upturned bucket in the stable doorway and listening to George's endless anecdotes.

" 'Course, we be very different types of folks, you be-in' Glaws and we be-in' Zummerset…"

But we were not very different. Red arrived back with the tired first horse, and soon I was listening to a vaudeville duo who, in the next few days, gave me a lifetime love of anecdote and oral history. I loved to listen and they loved an audience, and like their Greek antecedents they spoke of heroes and epics. How else would I know of the hunted stag that jumped into the sea off Porlock Hill and swam to South Wales? How else would the life of the great huntsmen of the 1920s, Ernest Bawden and Sidney Tucker, be recalled?

If Bawden was the Ajax of these tales, then Tucker was the Odysseus. Exmoor was over-populated with red deer in these years, and farmers felt the pressure in terms of broken fences and ruined crops. Tucker became a hero, famed equally for his knowledge of the moor as for his cunning as a hunter. But he was, like the Greek hero, flawed by pride, as this sample from the Red'n George recitations indicates:

> *Red*: Remember that day up above Dunkerley?
> *George*: Big patch o' gorse, right up aside the beacon
> *R*: Hot day, late season
> *G*: But those stags were strong
> Tucker found this 'un in Withypool
> Though some say 'twas Simonsbath
> But they all came up the beacon in a sweat…
> Men spent, hosses spent…
> Ten mile up and down
> Stag ran straight
> But he were finished too…
> When he saw the gorse.
> On to his knees like a burrowing animal.
> In 'e went, till it closed all over 'im
> Sea of gorse, no stag in sight

Hounds come up
And stop dead
No prickly gorse for them
Whipper in tries 'em
Not interested in whip or horn
Sidney comes up
'E wants to put his hoss in
But the creature ain't for it
Saving his lady-legs from the gorse
So Sidney gets angry
He tells them they're cowards
If you won't hunt stag
I will
So he's off his hoss
And tryin' to walk in hisself
But the gorse is too tall
And grown together…
So he has to go like the stag
Hands and knees
Thick hunting coat drawn over his 'ead
We watched
Sidney's backside going through the gorse
Sidney's curses on all of us for cowards
Then, of a sudden
The stag's head come up
Not ten foot ahead of Sidney's back
'E took a long look at that back
Then in a moment
He rose majestic like
Sprung through the air
Landed, four square
On Sidney's back

Then sprung again
Out of the gorse
Past us all
Away down the hill
None of us moved
Not 'ounds nor riders
We all turned
To pick up Sidney
'Is back hurt and…
He was sore, but
Most of all
He was angry wi' us
For not catching his stag

And there was much more in this Homeric vein. It was the perfect antidote to Father's captious complaints on his return. The moor, surprisingly, was open country. There were no fences to jump. You had to ride up and down steep hills very fast. His horses were too big – and unfit. Everyone else had mounts two hands smaller and very agile. It was not like the Cotswolds. Had it not been for the importance of establishing himself in the eyes of Captain Wallace as a fearless hunting man he would go home tomorrow.

Then I realised that I did not want to go. I was halfway through Rev Gleig and wanted to reach Waterloo at least before we left. I wanted more hours with my new friends in the stables. I was just learning, alongside Father, how to read a stag's antlers to tell its age. The old men gave us a set of antlers that sat for years on the barn wall at Evenlode and now grace the back wall of my house. While not "all his rights and seven-a-top" that a rare old stag would carry, this sixteen-pointer served as a school yard for two less able pupils. I enjoyed life in the hotel. Despite myself, despite my reservations, I was enjoying the weekend.

So I told Father that going home the next day would convince my mother that we could not manage without her, and who knew what further restrictions that might impose on him? He saw the point, driven home by a large whisky at the bar, and agreed to complete the plan with a further day on Monday. Which left Sunday for mutual entertainment. We asked the advice of Sean aka Anthony. He pointed out that for the impoverished, Minehead public golf course was free on Sunday mornings. In the spirit of Sidney Tucker, Father announced that he had seen golf on television. It was a simple, almost trivial game. He had seen Jack Nicklaus and Arnold Palmer. They hardly ever missed anything. He would certainly challenge me to a game.

The professional at the Minehead course was understanding and accommodating next day. He pointed out the strong offshore breeze, which he said would increase as the anticipated rain came in. He asked how often we played and when he learnt that we were complete novices recommended we buy a bucket full of used balls and treat the round as a practice. Father protested. He said all he needed was one ball and one of the sticks you used to hit it. But I had the purse and we followed the advice of the pro.

The outward nine followed the cliff top. Our best drives ended in the sea, the worst trickled down the cliff. On the return we lost the balance of our bucket in the stream, where local boys were already fishing them out for resale. By the time the rain arrived we were comfortably in the clubhouse bar. After lunch we were back in the stables, bringing a bottle of rum to reward the ostlers for horse care, and to prime them for the next rounds of oral history.

On Tuesday we drove home. We had not said a word all weekend about farming or succession. Insofar as we were together we had enjoyed each other's company. I had felt responsible for him for the first but not the last time. I had managed the money and had not had to cash the cheque provided by my mother for "emergencies". Father reported on the weekend as a triumph in terms of his objective. I was left wondering. If only I could persuade him of what I felt he half knew already – that I would never be a farmer – then we might even end up having a relationship of sorts, despite the fact that I had no interest in agriculture and hunting and horses, and he had little time or patience or toleration for anything else.

Chapter 20

Breakfast with Vinegar

ITHIN FARMING FAMILIES, like Jewish families, food can become ritual and in ours Father became "high priest of taste". The strong and skilful women who had prepared the food stood in silent apprehension while he tasted the first mouthful. The reaction would be pithy, never expressed in my early years with great enthusiasm, and produced relief or tension at the table. A "not bad, Kath" relaxed us all. A "had better", addressed to a woman who had worked five hours to lay this feast before us, created an atmosphere and constrained conversation. We ate only two types of meat dish: roast meat – pork, lamb, chicken or beef – and game. Fish was almost entirely confined to salmon (always cooked poached) when contacts on the Severn produced one. Turkey was reserved for Christmas. Game was usually a brace of pheasants – always on Father's birthday – partridges, or a haunch of venison sent across from the Duke's verderer.

Gran was the mistress of all things game and the authority on how they were to be cooked. My mother went on preparing game in Gran's style, since once an orthodoxy was established with Father there could be no subsequent variation. If there was a deviation and it was spotted then retribution followed –

"Don't want food that's been mucked about with…"

But the critical area of judgement around game concerned hanging, and here the high priest was in his element. He knew exactly how long the meat should be hung before it was eaten. As far as venison was concerned, deer should be hung skinned, by the back feet, and for up to three weeks. But you had to keep watch, for it could be shorter or longer, and everything depended on the time of year and the temperature. The idea was to make it tender and gamey in flavour. Or you could just make it rotten.

By contrast, pheasant was usually hung in its feathers. Traces of yellow decay in the leg socket were a sign that it was ready to eat, but Father had to approve hanging times, or he could come out with "could have done with a few more days" when we reached the vital point of taste arbitration. Roast meat joints were usually prepared the same way from the same cuts. Topside of beef was a perennial, and so was my mother's anxiety.

"Not too well done in the middle, Robs?"

"It'll do for now."

Did he really believe that his grudging praise and fault-finding improved standards and made his wife the very fine cook she was, as I once heard him claim in (male) company? He genuinely believed what his mother had told him, that he had a fine palate and an excellent ability to make judgements about food. It is easy to imagine that in her widowhood she turned him into the family head whose judgement in these things mattered, and since in the first fifty years of his life he did not encounter meat or fish cooked in any other way than described here, he became a taste tyrant.

We children, sitting around the dining room table at Nibley Farm when taste inquisition was taking place, cannot be blamed if we were a bit bemused by all of this. For we saw, with a sharpness that evaded the adults, exactly how Father prepared the food on his plate for eating. In the first instance, everything was covered with a generous layer of salt, and then pepper, making my mother sneeze. Then mustard came to the plate, accompanied by super-strong horseradish sauce in the case of beef. Other roasts invited other things, and the game came with redcurrant jelly and a strong port-wine sauce. Finally, over the top of everything, Father poured a generous helping of malt vinegar, and would sit before a cooling plate of food, unable to eat if no vinegar was available. His grandmother had taught him that without it food, especially vegetables, were totally tasteless.

The food was then sliced into very thin slices, mixing meat and veg judiciously, coated in mustard and dipped in the puddles of vinegar that had not yet soaked into his food. It was loaded carefully onto the back of the fork and taken up by the mouth with a snapping gesture, much like a horse taking a treat from the flat hand. While time-regulated chewing took place, the next mouthful was prepared with vigorous cutting and sorting and much noisy clashes of knife and fork. There was also time to instruct the children in the art of eating.

"Don't use the wrong side of the fork, devil take you."

"Less noise with those eating irons, you sound like gypsy children!"

Modern, fearless children would have called out the hypocrisy. We simply sat and wondered if he had burnt every taste bud out of his mouth through constant abuse. Years later I can speculate on food-taste approval as a control mechanism. For a man who, in every other domestic respect, was as helpless as a very small child, this may have been his only way of reasserting himself in the face of his wife's management.

Food requires preparation. In many respects the kitchen was a closed mystery to Father. The meat for roasting came from Stuart Hobbs, the butcher in Sodbury High Street. He was a valued friend and ally of my mother, but there was trouble if he provided an alternative to the favoured topside cut of beef, or if it wasn't aged sufficiently. It was a complicated relationship as well since he bought steers from us: a tense conversation in Yate market about tough meat improperly aged led to the rejoinder that the butcher intended to seek improved sources of supply. But it was also a friendly relationship, and I can recall the butcher buying some steers off the farm, and kindly showing me the favoured topside joint with a piece of chalk on one of the steers backsides before they were loaded up. Another supplier to the kitchen was Father himself, still the vegetable gardener of his youth. Complex processes were involved: soot from our chimneys went on the asparagus as well as manure, and rhubarb was never forced properly without Father's night-time attentions.

There were also pre-kitchen preparations to consider. Digging horseradish roots was one. Regularly sent on this Sunday-morning chore, it was almost always the case that the ones I dug were too old, and then, when younger, too small. Only Father could wash them in the old dairy beside the kitchen, then we would both stand at the sink and cut the roots into chips, tears running from our eyes within minutes.

From the kitchen window came the sound of *Two-Way Family Favourites* on the radio, which connected the occupying British troops in Germany with their families at home through music requests. This drowned our sobs while giving my sister Jane, working alongside my mother, a chance to hear her current favourites. If I listen hard I can still hear "Pickin' a Chicken" (Eve Boswell, 1956).

Another food preparation chore was in fact closely related. We all hated plucking pheasants, pulling the feathers from cold and always old birds. The feathers often resisted, bits of flesh came away, tough clumps needed a knife or scissors. Small wonder my mother covered the bird with bacon while cooking it. A chicken was different. My mother having requested one for Sunday lunch, I came across Father in the upper yard, surrounded by pullets which he had attracted by throwing down some corn. He was carrying the large metal bucket that invariably accompanied him round the yards. While the hens pecked gratefully, he eyed them with intent. He looked up as I arrived and explained his purpose. Did I shrug, or say "so what" or make some other juvenile ten-year-old's expression of indifference? All of a sudden he was a figure possessed. Turning his bucket upside down he adroitly dropped it on top of a plump bird directly in front of him. There was a slight squawk, the noise of wings flapping on metal, then silence. A finger pointed in my direction told me that I would play a role in the ensuing action.

Father raised one edge of the bucket and inserted a calloused hand covered in swart black hair. An oath told me he had been pecked. A cry of triumph followed as he swung the hen up in the air, holding it firmly by the legs. It was almost like the act of a manic magician. But unlike the doves appearing from a top hat, this episode ended sadly for the hen. One more turn through the air above his head and then Father brought her head done with a smart crack against the gatepost beside me. The hen now hung limp, gently dripping blood from its beak.

"Get the bucket," he said, and when I brought it, "Put it upside down and sit on it." He then thrust the bird into my hands. "The rewards of unseemly levity," he said. "Now pluck it!"

After the miseries of pheasant preparation, this seemed to me joyfully easy. A young bird and a warm one. I started on the breast first and the feathers came away easily, almost in handfuls. I was soon finished there, leaving feathers on neck and legs till last. I turned it over and blood dripped out on to my Wellington boots. Again, leaving the wings and tail until last, I came rapidly down the bird's back. I will soon be finished here, I thought, and that will show him. Then I thought I felt movement, or was it just the dead bird slipping on my lap? And then I did feel movement as our lunch, merely stunned, leapt from my lap and started cavorting around the yard. With feathers at neck, wing and feet, but otherwise nude, it looked like a jerky, earlycartoon film as it raced away, half running, half flying. I was lumbering in hot pursuit by the time Father arrived. After some pithy observations to the effect that my abilities at plucking matched my other agricultural and domestic skills, we cornered the runaway together and I was soon back on the bucket plucking the remainder of a now headless bird.

This episode and others helped to persuade Father that I was "not up to man's work", and at ten he was probably right. I was certainly glad to be a bystander at the last, and never-repeated, attempt to cure our own bacon. Father wanted to return to the 1930s when, he said, this had been a normal household chore. My mother was not keen, but Father pointed out that we had the ideal place, a stone-flagged cold room in the depths of the house which had been built for this purpose even if it was now used as a children's playroom. My first thought was where the table-tennis table would go. My mother rightly insisted that if this had to be, the slaughtering had to be done professionally.

And it had to be done. Father could no longer think or speak of anything else. A return to the wonderful bacon of his childhood was on hand, accompanied by flavours that I could not possibly imagine, since I had never tasted "real bacon". No one like me, brought up on such shoddy products as Stuart Hobbs's home-cured or Harris of Calne's shop-bought (often made from our pigs) could possibly imagine what bacon tasted like. He was about to turn the clock back and an important part of our education was about to take place. So I was deeply interested when two men arrived from Pucklechurch with a large tank which we filled with water and set up above a burner in the yard. The burner was lit and stoked with logs, and after a long wait we had merrily boiling water. One of the more mature and heavier of the baconers was brought around from the Tump. Now came the horror story, so loud and affecting that even Father never dared to repeat it.

The pig had to have its throat cut while it was slipped into the boiling water. This was apparently to burn away the swart hairs on the pig's back so that they should not appear in the rind. In order to accomplish this vital task, Father and two of our men, Chris and Gerald, were drafted in to pick up the pig and hold it above the water. They were joined by one of the slaughtermen to give one person on each leg while the senior slaughterman prepared the throat-cutting knives.

The pig was strong and struggled. The tank, once on the burner, was at an awkward height and the men struggled. The pig started to touch the water before the throat-cutting could be completed. The noise. No one who heard it could ever forget it. It tore through our brains until we were deaf. My mother rushed indoors holding her head. We were held in a version of the Munch *Scream*.

Then it was over. The dead pig wallowed in the water. The slaughtermen heaved him out with meat hooks, took off his head, cut him in half from tail to neck, and soon the two halves were hanging by the back legs and draining blood. And in a day or two my role in this pantomime materialised. Father appeared with a box of salt blocks, like huge bars of carbolic soap. Since my bedroom was just above the old playroom, wouldn't it be a simple thing for me, last thing at night and first thing in the morning, to thoroughly rub each side with salt? Ten or fifteen minutes each side would do. He was sure others would help, but it really was just the job for a child.

I quite liked being alone in the playroom with these great, cold, swinging sides of meat, and the salt-rubbing was not onerous. But however much I washed my hands, the salt, burning in every tiny cut or abrasion on my hands, kept me awake at night and made it hard to hold a pen at school. My mother took me off the rota and the curing process was completed by her vigorous household help, Mrs Roberts. The end result was bacon, not as good as Uncle Dick's similar experiment at the same time or, we thought, as good as Hobbs the butcher, but definitely eatable bacon. Father did not do post-mortems. He just moved on.

It seemed to me that every table of food was full of things I had never "really" tasted. Father was also a brand champion. You quickly discovered this if you served him the wrong goods. Did we not know that there was only one marmalade, Frank Cooper's Oxford Vintage, and everyone else's was an attempt at passing off? Colman's was the only mustard: any claim that mustard could come from France was particularly pernicious. How dare people pretend that their "foreign muck" should have the noble name of mustard appended to it?

It was the same with places. It could not be a pork pie unless it came from Melton Mowbray. Since he proudly repeated that a day spent five miles from his front door was a day wasted, and even in restaurants he never ate anything that my mother might not have cooked (and then said "not as good as yours, Kath" – he knew the required diplomacy) his culinary experience was limited. Apart from a coach trip to Austria and Germany with the National Farmers Union to view farms, he never travelled until my sister Mary and I took him to Ireland, of which more later.

But it would be wrong to suggest that Father's taste hegemony stopped at roast lunches on Sunday. It ran to every meal and from morning until night, and it was always accompanied by ritual. Mary and I would watch transfixed as the ceremony of the morning cereal, as complex and ordered as the Changing of the Guard, took place. Nobody could do this for him. The quantities of material and their precise ordering in the stack built up in his breakfast bowl were matters that only he could accomplish. First into his great bowl went the prunes, the "little black workers" that were important for regularity and peace of mind. I hear the voice of his mother here. Once the prunes had been de-stoned, and the stones arranged in an orderly manner on the lip of the plate, the prunes were mashed into a pulp in their rich juices. There were never less than five and often more. There then followed a layer of cornflakes, covering the prunes completely to a depth of at least half an inch. Then came the stewed fruit, which could have been anything that my mother had available. Then came the cream, covering and soaking everything and providing a lake upon which was poured the oats. Horseman and steed had dietary crossovers. Onto the oats and covering them went a further layer of cornflakes, and this time a tablespoonful of sugar was added to satisfy the maestro's taste buds. At length, he was ready to add milk, and having done so consumed the result noisily, taking care to ensure that each large spoonful cut down through and sampled each and every layer.

In the 1950s, and understandably given long days of manual labour, with morning milking already finished, this was followed by a full English breakfast, lavishly slathered with full-strength mustard and vinegar on the grilled tomatoes and mushrooms. Then toast and the famous marmalade. Tea, not coffee, was the preferred drink. In later years, with some of his burdens lifted in the North Cotswolds, breakfast could be followed by a short but noisy sleep in the armchair. Around 11 a.m. it was time for a "livener". Like a man preparing a religious ritual, two inches of Gordon's London Gin was poured into a pint mug and then filled to the top with Bulmer's Cider Perry. Only the pear-based drink would do. The dosage was repeated at 4 p.m. Despite repeated enquiries he could not explain how this began. He could misleadingly describe it as "just a glass of Perry" if asked. He would also claim not to be a beer drinker, though in earlier years he displayed a fondness for Worthington's India Pale Ale, one of the few bottled beers that continued to ferment and mature in the bottle.

The late 1950s were a period of rapid change in food tastes. Rationing finally ended in 1954. Import restrictions were lifted and new foods became available – and the British exhibited sudden passions for something new. The Danes not only sent their bacon and captured the British market, but they introduced lager beers. Young farmers divided between the competing camps of Tuborg and Carlsberg, and then moved on to sample, and eventually reject, the keg beers that followed the success of Watney's Red Barrel. Father was unimpressed (he referred to the lagers as "goat piss"), and in any case, needing to have beer and cider available by the barrel for casual harvesters and the threshing teams, knew that the only place to get what was required was Wadsworths of Devizes. Not the 6X, or no work would be done, yet keeping these reliable short-term labourers sweet was important.

Farmers no longer went to the Mop, the traditional employment fairs in Sodbury High Street where harvesting gangs had been engaged in the pre-war years and for generations before. Mechanization meant that you could get by with a much smaller workforce. Add sons-in-law to the regular workforce, rope in so-and-so's cousin who has just come out of the army and doesn't have a job yet, and one or so more and we could get by at a pinch, if the binder kept going, or later if the combine could cope without breakdowns and the baler held up before the rain came.

Father knew that it was important to meet the expectations of his workers – and of his guests.

When his best man's brother, Bill Brownsey, a Borneo timber merchant, came for the evening, my mother was asked to put a full bottle of whisky, and a carafe of water with a glass, on a small table beside his chair. I watched with fascination as the whisky level fell through the evening until I was sent to bed. When I checked in the kitchen in the morning there were only two fingers (child-size) left. His brother Bob was a great brandy drinker, and so was Mr Williams the seed merchant. Father could drink either, and had a great liking for port, which often went into one of the hunting hip flasks.

But there is also a secret truth, or perhaps a saving grace, concerning Father and alcohol. He had a very poor head. When he reached his limit he had a headache or fell asleep. Either event ended the intake. He could be very noisy on very little, however, prone to impromptu speeches or imitations of Josef Locke singing about sweet Kathleen or "the Mountains o' Mourne". While for his children he was becoming interesting at this point, such behaviour was very embarrassing to his wife, who soon put a stop to matters. Years later I tried to share with him an interest in good-quality wines.

He swigged them down by the glass and then said, "Where's the kick?"

Not for him the gentle and stimulatory effects of a vintage Bordeaux. He wanted what he called a "lift", a mind- and mood-changing experience even if he eventually passed out.

Chapter 21

Judgement Day

"JUDGE NOT LEST ye be judged." Father loved a biblical
quotation and this was one of his favourites. Delivered
sententiously, chin brought down in emphasis, the forefinger was raised at the listener for a long moment to allow the
true import of the words uttered to sink in. These quotations
were intended as conversation stoppers: game, set and match
in a conversation in which Father had triumphed by bringing
his long-dead great-aunt and grandmother as well as Moses
into the room to hurl back the blasphemers and win the day.

Yet no one was ever as judgemental as Father. The require-
ment of a farmer, to rate and value livestock, and his need
as a dealer in horses to do the same, became a habit of mind

with him. When he extended it to people, he could reach quite devastating judgements alarmingly quickly.

"They will never make anything of themselves," a favoured line of judgement, could be applied after an exposure of two sentences.

All of this arose from livestock and the sale ring. Of the three brothers, Father grew up as the one with the judgement of animals, and everyone deferred to that judgement just as they deferred in his household to his claims to know and judge good food. These family predilections became entrenched as family facts. His brother John chafed under their mother's insistence that Father should buy all the stock for his brother's new tenancy, as we have seen. When a cow bought this way was barren, or a calf died, John was quick to point out who had made the buying decision. No such problem existed with his youngest brother, Dick, who knew all about tractors and machinery, and thus was very safe from Father's interests and judgements.

Judgemental acts required from Father a special stance and often special noises. My sisters accompanied him to the Leicester Horse Repository for the hunter sales more often than I before the building in Belgrave Gate was demolished in 1960. My memories of two visits are marked by recall of the discomfort of riding in the cab of the lorry, and of the impressive arch at the front of the building. But then, and on many other occasions, I noted the special stance of the judge: knees slightly bent, half crouching, looking closely at the horse's belly before diving forward to seize the rear fetlock of one of the horse's legs, and abruptly pulling it off the ground. Subsequently, I was told that sudden was best since the equine subject might have other ideas on the matter, and that few horses could kick you with one foot off the ground.

Once he had that fetlock off the ground the questioning of the seller could begin. Any lameness? Cannon-bones fired? Osselets? Pastern bone swelling? Then a quick inspection of the hoof itself. The leg and foot of a horse, front and back, were, according to Father, the scene of so much potential disaster in terms of future lameness and loss of resale value that until you had looked at them and made a judgement there was no point in going further.

If you were reasonably satisfied then you next addressed the teeth and mouth.

"How old did you say this horse was?"

The practised long look of disbelief that followed reminded the neutral onlooker that judging a horse was in reality two parallel processes: forming one's own judgement of the animal's worth while destroying or at least undermining the seller's notion of the attainable price. Father was very good at both of these. Price disbelief should be set alongside the Unworthy Buyer Act noted earlier.

We should also note the role of incidental noises during judging processes. Placing his tongue on the roof of his mouth, closing his teeth and expelling air rhythmically through his lips, Father produced a sound which would have been extraordinary in anyone else, though it was quite typical of him. Why? I really wish I could explain this behaviour. Was it a mark of very extreme concentration? An indicator that he could not now be interrupted? A way of destroying further the confidence of the seller? Just something he did when he wasn't doing something else? A way of reassuring the horse that his intentions were not evil? A way of preventing the seller from asking questions that Father did not want to answer? Or an unconscious combination of all of these? I always took it that he was happy when emitting this noise, and similar noises could accompany shoeing (owing to lack of reliable access to a farrier, Father became his own amateur blacksmith), grooming, or other horse-related activities.

A sign that judging was nearly complete came when he asked for the horse to be led up and down in front of him. This could involve the owner or groom making several passes in front of him, spurred on by vigorous hand gestures and sometimes,

"Make him trot."

Eventually he straightened up. A decision had been reached. Now the seller had to prise it out of him. This would take time, and any admission of virtue in the animal could be grudging. The question of whether the horse was being sold with a vet's warranty could be critical. If yes, the counter could be,

"Then you won't mind my man having a look?"

If no, then why not? If the horse was warranted "sound in wind and limb" then what was that noise Father could hear when it trotted? If it had never been lame was that a swelling he felt in the pastern? As Father did in his role when a seller, vehement denials were given and ignored. Was the horse broken in Ireland? Would that explain why it would not let Father touch its ears? The point, I realised, was not to get to money talk quickly, since this elongated delay further loosened seller resolve.

Horses were always sold in guineas. Father believed that this was because transactions about horses, conducted by gentle-men, would never be resolved in common pounds sterling. The ungentlemanly behaviour of many buyers and most sellers did not dissuade him from this argument. Nor was he moved by my reminder of the link between the term guineas and the slave trade. But he was strongly aware, amidst all of the histrionics that he brought to judging, and then continued into selling, that dealing in anything was more of an art than a science.

He explained to me several times that each horse had two

"values". One, of course, was the value expressed in terms of the price anyone would pay for it. Whenever I asked what that price should be the answer came back like a shot:

"The lowest price you can get, and only pay that if you are absolutely sure that you can find a fool who will pay you more than you paid."

So what, then, was the second value?

Ah, well, that was what the horse was really worth, if rated against its peers. Father rarely had the experience of judging horses against each other at agricultural shows, and regarded it as an artificial exercise at best. But in his mind he considered what horseflesh he was looking at in the light of the many horses he had bought and sold.

It seemed to me with hindsight many years later that here was a very Aristotelian concept, as if Father had in his head a picture of the Horse, a definition, a template, an archetype against which all of the horses that he judged might be compared – and marked down. He was fond of the paintings of George Stubbs, and when I said that those arched necks and tails looked artificial, he said that to him they looked too perfect – just how horses should have looked – and were obviously painted that way to flatter the owner and allow the painter to ease his price up a bit. Father, though unworldly about handling money, was very commercial when it came to attaining it.

In less exaggerated performance than horse judging, the same thinking was applied to other forms of livestock judging. During my efforts to make it as a pig judge and impress him, I learnt from trying to place four pigs in a pen into an order of merit that there was one factor that I came back to time and again. The judges who judged the contestants had a word for it. They called it "conformation". You had to see the animal move to get this into perspective. Like people, cows or pigs could be graceful or awkward. Some had body parts seemingly in exact proportion to each other. As such a beast walked, the joints seemed to make these proportionate limbs flow together in an easy gait. Others looked as if they had been constructed of spare, leftover parts. Ridges of fat or muscle marked the junction of limbs and joints. Walking was uneven, favouring one leg or one side. Gently moving my pigs around the stye I became a student of physical harmony. (I do not think, incidentally, that I was better at spotting those factors than the other judges in the competition. I was just better at presentation and had more words to describe what I saw.)

Father clearly recognised this concept. Years later, when we had Hereford steers at Evenlode, we leant on the fence and compared them in these terms. He asserted that better conformation produced more valuable animals, and that this ran right through to meat on the bone and value in the carcass. Conscious of it or not, breeders bred to the better conformation factor wherever they could.

Whether this was true or not, it intrigued me that he felt the need for an intellectual logic behind the judging and breeding business. It wasn't just the flattery and shadow play of the dealer/spieler. He needed to know where all of this was leading and, since he made no pretence of any great religious belief, nor did he think he had a sacred duty to feed the nation, the idea that he was breeding and buying to encourage breeding directed towards the idea of producing a better animal was satisfying to him. In day-to-day dealings it probably meant little. In reflective moments, when he wondered at the advancement of the human race in material terms during his lifetime, it was his nod to the great Gods of Progress and Productivity.

Every great theoretician meets his Waterloo. Father's came in a village pub in the hills about twenty miles south of Limerick.

On one of his two overseas excursions, as we shall see later, he came with my sister Mary and myself on a hunting man's Irish odyssey.

Having crossed the country we had come down from the Rock of Cashel and were aiming to cross the Shannon and stay at the Bunratty Castle Hotel. But the day ran out on us, as Irish days so often do, and we got hungry and tired of driving. A village pub seemed the appropriate idea. Father, by then in his seventies, wanted a sleep. We went into the bar for a drink and a sleep. We ended up eating dinner and, since it was a feast washed down with beer and whiskey, we finished in the public bar enjoying the lively conviviality which informs such places. There we met the two brothers, and within a few moments they had Father's love of horses out on the table and were fondling it affectionately.

"And would you be thinking of doing a little dealing while you are amongst us, Mr Worlock?" opened a gate. "We have horses in this parish as can leap turf banks, and would just step over any fence in Gloucestershire" took a susceptible visitor through it. And "We have a horse ourselves that we really want your opinion on, you being such a skilful judge, and we are bringing him up the road to the paddock behind the pub before closing time so you can give us a view" baited the trap, just as "Why, we don't want to sell him, but for a connoisseur of your standing we could of course make an exception" flashed warning signs at everyone around the table except the connoisseur himself.

Meanwhile, while we waited for the horse to come up from the farm: "A little more Jameson's? Some more of the black stuff?"

Full of Guinness and whiskey we eventually stagger outside, bringing the rest of the bar with us. Into the headlights of the ring of cars around the paddock, the two brothers do indeed appear like a pair of leprechauns, small and gingery, twinkling and cunning. I have lost my ability to determine which one is Sean and which one is Pat, which one is the ex-jockey and which one has a business delivering supplies to stables around the county. And it does not really seem to matter, as they propel Father forward towards the fine bay gelding in the centre of the crowd. Its distinctly thoroughbred carriage is impressive even to me, as Father is beginning his judging routine. First the bending and the observation of the horse's belly. Then the walking around the horse. Now the familiar noises of air being expelled through pursed lips. The rush to seize a fetlock follows, and the back leg inspection commences. Then the horse is walked up and down until the judge nods his satisfaction. And then Father looks up.

"Remarkable how cool these cannon-bones are – no problems here then?"

"Sound as a bell!" came the reply.

Father is already checking the mouth. "What age?" he asks.

"About eight," comes the reply.

"About right," he responds.

Then he steps back, a forthcoming pronouncement of great import written on his face. The pub crowd falls silent.

"I have examined many horses in my time," says Father, "but very few have had the character and distinction of this one. Without hesitation I can say that this animal would fetch a premium price at Leicester or any of our English horse sales, subject to warranty. I would need to know if the horse could jump."

The brothers look pleased at an expected result, and gratified to hear it publicly announced. They quickly move to reassure the judge.

"In his younger days he won prizes," said Pat, or perhaps it was his brother.

"Would you like us to put a saddle on him so you can just see what a Rolls Royce ride he is?" says the other.

We have reached that hour just before midnight when a man who has drunk not wisely but well can do anything suggested by anyone.

"Of course," said Father, to the horror of his children.

I step forward to point out that he had no jodhpurs, that it would be better to do this in daylight, that they have no jumps in the paddock ... but I am shushed into silence, and I hear Sean, or maybe it was Pat, saying,

"They have a lot of boxes back of the bar. Let's make a little jump."

I am consumed by the thought of what I would say to my mother, who entrusted Father to me for a fortnight, if he met an untimely end falling off in an Irish paddock while under the influence.

It takes a little while to get Father into the saddle but once he is there he looks very professional. He walks the horse up and down and everything looks great. My confidence is returning, as Sean / Pat says,

"Put him at this little fence, willya, Mr Worlock?"

Father puts the horse into a trot, and we observers are aware of some awkwardness in the horse's gait, but the rider is oblivious. The "fence" is indeed little: just a single line of cardboard boxes.

The horse is turned towards the target, effort expended with knees, heels and sound effects to create impulsion and thus conquer the small barrier. With effort the horse achieves a fast trot and runs through the boxes, scattering them in all directions and hitting a pole placed across the top of them with a loud clang. Father, fearing damage, dismounts hurriedly.

By now the paddock was full of laughing villagers, many

more than were within the pub to begin with. The barman stood outside the back door of the pub, arms akimbo, and remarked to me that it always drew a good crowd when someone tried to ride The Tin Man. Slowly we strangers were caught up with the story of a quality racehorse, loved by the brothers, that went lame and had metal splints inserted by a vet in Waterford in a desperate but unsuccessful attempt to save its career.

"But those cannon-bones was cool, wasn't they, Mr Worlock?" I heard Sean, but it may have been Pat, say as we returned to the bar, where the drinks were on us.

By morning the incident did not seem in the least discreditable, and Father acknowledged the greetings of the residents like a visiting dignitary as we strolled in the village before taking our leave.

All judges are fallible – Father would have been the first to acknowledge this – and many judges are motivated less by loftier considerations than by the need to get the price right. Father himself provided an illustration of a perfect judge at work in one of his many letters to the hunting press:

HORSE AND HOUND
February 9, 1963

A Month's Frost

SIR. Way back in the bad farming years of the early thirties I had a young horse that I was too busy to hunt. I asked the late Mr Herbert Nell to come and bid me for him.

He duly arrived in his smart pony and trap and the inspection began. He remarked, "Not a bad sort if it were not for his ewe neck, and straight shoulder, but of course he's got a back as long as a month's frost. I'll give you 25 Guineas for him."

I never forgot the remark or the price but a good upbringing forbade me to enquire if he proposed to pay in a lump sum!

W. R. G. WORLOCK

Chapter 22

A Man of Letters

FATHER WAS IN LOVE with books but, especially in the years of extensive manual labour, was not always in love with reading. There was always a dog-eared tome on the little table beside his armchair, but I could never understand how he could seemingly open the book at random, or at one of several folded-down pages and commence grazing with great equanimity.

When I questioned this practice in later years he said mildly that a good book tasted good wherever you sampled it, but this habit does at least explain why he was unsure of plot and denouement of any of the fictional works he claimed to have read. It also explains why his enduring favourite was the very episodic *Pickwick Papers*. He would have been an ideal Victorian-serial reader.

It is probable that his earliest reading mentors were readers of such serials. His grandmother and great-aunt first of all taught the boy to know and love his Bible. The King James Version of the Old Testament is our linguistic and cultural bedrock, and all his life Father was able to quote extensively from it. Father had a stock of pithy quotes all delivered with a knowing finality, a certainty that they closed the argument. There would be a short pause. Then, the last crushing blow as he spat out the biblical source: Kings, Ecclesiastes, Judges. His expression plainly read "Now get out of that one!"

Or the quotation may have been followed by the word "Spurgeon". The two old ladies were devotees of the sermons of the Prince of Preachers, Charles Haddon Spurgeon. The Cotswold villages had a long love affair with great preachers, from George Whitfield and the Wesley brothers onwards. Spurgeon was beloved not just by Baptists. Though it is perhaps doubtful whether either of Father's instructors ever heard him speak, either in the New Park Street Chapel or amongst the 10,000 who attended his great Southwark meetings, they certainly loved a sermon, and left Father with a firm impression of Spurgeon's position as a final authority on what Christianity meant.

Sadly for the two old ladies, Father was not a Christian. As we have noted, he did believe in Providence and had a great understanding of the need to help others in distress. He often said that when the moment comes "you know the right thing to do." So those two elderly ladies, who took charge of the half-orphaned boy who may not have seen much of his mother through these years, did not succeed in implanting their own rather narrow religious beliefs. But perhaps they did something better, as they read to him and encouraged him to read. They gave him a sense of morality that never left him, and the memory of a book that encased that morality in the mid-nineteenth-century setting in which it was created.

The two ladies were keen readers of the novels of Diana Mulock, more often referred to as Mrs Craik. In an age of great female writers like Mrs Gaskell, Charlotte Brontë and especially George Eliot, she is largely unknown today. Her moral stories are important in one sense that is not always recognised however: her work, alongside that of Harriet Beecher Stowe, persuaded the Baptists of Tresham and elsewhere that it was permissible to read fiction. Of course, given licence to read such "improving" literature as Mrs Craik produced, the non-conformists of the villages were exposed to other ideologies carried in the same bloodstream. Mrs Craik's great best-seller was published three years before Samuel Smiles's classic, *Self-Help*, and she pre-empted the theme of that hugely successful and influential book.

Mrs Craik herself was very successful. The novel that so influenced Father, his grandmother and great-aunt was called *John Halifax, Gentleman*. Published in 1857, it came second only in popularity to *Uncle Tom's Cabin* in the following decade. Those two books, with *The Pilgrim's Progress*, were described by Father as "the great books on which I was brought up" and thus, whenever in later years I raved about something that moved me, the admonishing forefinger went up:

"But *John Halifax, Gentleman*, Dave – it can't compare to that!"

Those who seek to read the book today may find that a hundred and fifty years of adverse literary criticism cannot all be wrong. But if it is devoid of much literary value, it has huge historical significance. John Halifax is a penniless, orphaned farm labourer, whose kindly acts towards Phineas Fletcher, the son of his boss, as well as his own dedicated hard work raise him up to unostentatious prosperity. Phineas narrates the story, which begins in the 1780s, and shows how John masters first water power and then steam to bring prosperity to the town of Enderley. Marrying Ursula, an heiress, against her father's wishes, he has to succeed without her dowry. In bad times he feeds the starving workforce, in good he is the beneficent master and magistrate. All he inherited from his father was a Greek Testament, which was his grandfather's and showed the family came from "good blood".

Now let us overlay this story on Father's own life and it is hard not to see parallels. Despite agricultural disasters, recessions, pandemics and depressions that had scarred the family history, the self-help and Protestant work ethic remained strong in the Cotswold valleys. You were expected to fend for yourself and struggle out of difficulty through effort. John Halifax was an innovator, and so was Father, though machine-averse. He was always keen to try a new crop or a new ley or a new breed. Like John, he was an arch-romantic (with some mental but not actual slippages). Like John, he knew he came from "good stock", as he would have put it, but he was born at a difficult time for his family. Small wonder that John Halifax and his story remained a touchstone for him all his life. In his seventies he could recall John's proposal to Ursula, and the local election where John urged his men to vote freely with their consciences and ignore the bribes of evil Lord Luxmore.

These books had a profound influence on his formative years, and stayed with him. At school, and especially at Wycliffe, other things came along that were important to his sense of being an educated man, but perhaps did not get so close to the man himself.

"Nobody wrote anything to better Scott and Dickens" would not be a fashionable view today, but was gospel to him. He bought a complete set of Dickens from a country house sale but never, I think, broke the back of any of them. Apart from *Pickwick*

Papers, he showed a good knowledge of *David Copperfield*. He probably knew *The Old Curiosity Shop* as well, since he used to read us the passages covering the death of Little Nell.

As it ended:

She was dead. No sleep so beautiful and calm, so free from trace of pain, so fair to look upon. She seemed a creature fresh from the hand of God, and waiting for the breath of life; not one who had lived and suffered death … Dear, gentle, patient, noble Nell was dead.

He would look up, satisfaction in his face if his children had dissolved in tears or fled the room, and his wife was begging him to desist.

He produced the same effect with recitations of "The Place Where the Old Horse Died". In time he only had to start:

> In the hollow, by the pollard, where the crop is tall and rank
>> Of the dock leaf and the nettle growing free,
> Where the bramble and the brushwood straggle blindly o'er
>> the bank,
>> And the Pyat jerks and chatters on the tree…

and he knew we would be emotionally broken by the time he reached:

>> For never man had friend
>> More enduring to the end,
> Truer mate in every turn of time and tide.
>> Could I think we'd meet again
>> It would lighten half my pain
> At the place where the old horse died.

And he was always right. I do not think he read these things to us to educate or entertain. He just liked us to cry, perhaps evoking tears of his own that had been long suppressed.

Of Scott he had retained less, perhaps, than Dickens. "Lochin-var" was a favourite poem, chanted while rhythmically swaying from side to side. In the best Chapel traditions he loved hymns (and, like his mother, funerals: "Abide with Me" topped the charts for both of them). Father caused his family deep embarrassment when we were all forced into a church for formal occasions: his descant followed the trebles up to the roof timbers and well beyond the scope of his light baritone. There is no doubt, however, that he got genuine pleasure from reciting and singing. Though he always had to be forced to perform, there was a performer lurking inside him, and it took only a small whisky to tease him out. In later years we often read "Lochinvar" and "Sir Patrick Spens" aloud. At this time I bought him the Kingsley Amis collection published as *The Faber Popular Reciter*: after his death I found it broken with use, rebound in sellotape, still beside his chair.

The hymns of Isaac Watts brought back his childhood with immediacy, and Clough's "Say not the Struggle Naught Availeth" was a watchword. But though I tried hard to infect him with a passion I had for Yeats and Rudyard Kipling, I had to read them alone from this book. But we did get pleasure from Arnold Silcock's joyful collection, *Verse and Worse*, introduced to the family when it served my sister Mo and I as our sanity resource during a mad weekend spent trying to sell crisps and soft drinks to holidaymakers from a traditional gypsy caravan in a lay-by on the A465.

And the *Reciter* introduced Thomas Babington Macaulay, via "Horatius". Once we had crossed that bridge and I had found a copy of *Lays of Ancient Rome*, we settled on a firm favourite: "The Battle of Naseby by Obadiah Bind-his-kings-in-chains-and-his-nobles-in-links-of-iron" really appealed. The political message was perhaps lost on him, but he loved the victory of the just and, a strong characteristic, he loved language and interesting words.

He always stopped at the description of Charles I:

...the Man of Blood was there, with his long essenced hair.

He pronounced the three syllables of the adjective with special relish.

Scott, then, was an author who he had heard about and whose reputation had to be respected, and Father swore by *Ivanhoe*, yet plainly had only the sketchiest idea of what it was about. He once told me that the only book to compare with *John Halifax* was *Heart of Midlothian*, and in later years I bought him a copy to refresh his memory. Years later he confessed that he had found it unreadable.

In the same category could be placed Samuel Johnson. Father had been taught from *Lives of the Poets*. In the curious way of English education, this meant that he had retained some knowledge of fifty-two minor eighteenth-century poets but, like modern English children whose world history is the Tudors and the First World War, the rest of the canvas was a blank.

He thus shared Johnson's tenderness for Thomas Gray, whose "Elegy in a Country Churchyard" he admired, but he had a received impression of the Great Cham's omniscience that Johnson himself would have liked immensely. By the same token, Father's best man, Bob Brownsey, had given him a copy of Boswell's *London Journal*, saying it was "very racy". Father searched it high and low, and then gave it to me when I was a schoolboy. He said that he was damned if he could find the dirty bits but maybe I might have better luck.

I read it, and fell in love with the crisis-driven uncertainties of the young diarist who wanted nothing to do with the life that his father had mapped out for him. In the next decade I collected the rest of the letters and diaries in the wonderful Yale edition, ever grateful for the introduction but still not finding the lubricious content sought by those two surprisingly well-read farmers. Again, later, I was able to give Father a copy of both writers' Highland tours in one volume, which altered his view of them entirely.

So Father was a well-read man, better educated than many farmers of his time. He had no science or technology, and preferred to let my mother bother with the vital arithmetic, ceding the farm accounts to her entirely. He was always reading something by way of a book, and often several at the same time. While politics and religion did not much concern him in maturity (he followed a line of peaceful non-resistance to my mother's strong views on these subjects), we always had a daily newspaper (the *News Chronicle*, then the *Daily Telegraph*, and latterly and deplorably, the *Daily Mail*). Weekly came the *Wilts and Gloucester Standard*, a valued source of local news, "I read it in the *Standard*" giving events near Biblical veracity. Father's often-stated ambitions concerned both of these publications:

"I want to be worth a million in the Wills column of the *Telegraph*" and "I want to be buried in the *Standard*."

It is sad to reflect that he achieved neither, but it was not for want of hoping. And did they not owe him something? After all, he must have written hundreds of letters to newspapers and magazines, though a particular target in the latter category was the weekly *Horse and Hound*. On its cover it boasted a commendation from the Victorian novelist and hunting enthusiast, George Whyte-Melville. Father pored over its pages with great enthusiasm when it arrived and penned hopeful letters, like the one quoted above, for publication.

Whyte-Melville, as we have seen, wrote sentimental doggerel about dead horses. He himself died in the hunting field in 1878. He had moved to Tetbury in the 1870s, living at Barton Abbott's, only a few miles from Father's birthplace at Calcot Manor, so that he could be closer to the good hunting afforded by the Beaufort and the Vale of the White Horse. Often known as the author of the poem beginning "To eat drink and be merry, because tomorrow we die", he is a contemporary of R. S. Surtees. Father was a great fan of John Jorrocks, Soapy Sponge, James Pigg and Mr Facey Romford and the gallery of hunting hopefuls who crowd Surtees's pages, but although he owned a ten-volume set of Whyte-Melville classics, I do not recall him ever quoting them and indeed he may never have read them.

His curiosity about the use and misuse of words was endless. Back in 1955 I recall it as a constant cause of domestic disharmony. Father, writing one of his copious notes to friends and relatives, would ask my mother if he was using the right word. She would then look it up in her dictionary, the typist's dictionary that had lain beside her typewriter in the law office of Burges Salmon. She then produced an answer which, if it did not satisfy the writer, was disputed. He was then told it was in the dictionary, so that was final. The veracity of the dictionary was then questioned. After all, it was not *Oxford* or *Collins*. This infuriated my mother, who returned to the kitchen promising never to help such an annoying person ever again. Her impatience was justified: when he knew he was right then he was right, even when he was wrong. As an adult I bought him an *Oxford Dictionary* to try to even things up, but immediately regretted it since it put my mother's nose out of joint. Was I joining Father in suggesting that her dictionary was somehow wrong? What on Earth was I suggesting when I said words changed their meaning or new words came along? Her dictionary had served her well throughout the 1930s and was still her authoritative guide now. She also had her schoolgirl *Phillip's Atlas* which was produced to settle disputes about boundaries and capital cities. I tactfully refrained from replacing that, even when I worked for a publisher that produced a far more modern one.

In this household where words mattered, Father wrote thousands of them every month. More as he grew older, more in the summer, less in the hunting season. In later years he kept a hunting diary, though its entries are haphazard and sometimes stop at the weather. Postcards were a favourite medium, with the writing, still a lineal descendent of the copperplate he had been taught at school, getting smaller and smaller as more thoughts crowded in that had to be communicated in this word dump. Sadly, some of this heritage is now very hard to decipher, but examples have been quoted here.

Like me, many of his correspondents kept his letters. When you received one, you knew you had been written to with a vengeance. Here were no trivial enquiries. If he meant to flatter you, then you got the full trowelful. He often employed archaic speech forms: for the Duke of Marlborough, or Ronnie Wallace, or his great friend and fan, Charm Fleming of Leygore, it must have been like receiving a letter posted in the 1830s. They enjoyed it and responded in kind.

He did not write to get a response. He wrote driven by an urge that had to be satisfied. Sometimes you would get three postcards in a week, then nothing for three weeks. Was he making up in these later years for earlier ones which were barren of any communication at all? During my years at school he never wrote at all. What is certain is that his career as a man of letters, in full flow once he reached the safe haven of Evenlode, brought pleasure and anxiety to many as they got out their magnifying glasses to pore over the tiny words, only to turn the page to find the script had ballooned out to twenty-four point, with florid letters adorned with swirls and curlicues not seen since the handwriting manuals of the pre-1914 period. If you saw your name in those letters on the envelope you knew you were in for a treat – and possibly a puzzle.

Chapter 23

Two Women and a Pony

A S I WALKED AWAY from the headmaster's house after the definitive meeting to "decide" my future, I might have been feeling triumphant that I had made everyone, and especially Father, think, and forced another year. Perhaps I felt some anger with my mother who had left me to face Father and the headmaster on my own. But the victory I felt was a victory of my own making. It took almost ten years of armed co-existence before I fully realised the cost of that victory for Father, for me and for our relationship. We found it harder and harder to talk, and we certainly could not roll up our several discontents with each other into some confrontational moment. Since we could not "have it out", we inevitably grew further and further apart. Neither of us could see how much we were hurting each other.

For me, this apartness was very easy to manage. Since I had had it drummed into me that I was of no earthly use to man or beast unless I could be a farmer, it was easy to take this literally. I had lived with the idea slowly forming inside me that I was not going to be a farmer since I was ten or eleven. Now I had a chance of self-determination, I was not going to give it up just because it did not fit with the pre-conceptions of others on how my life might be lived. I saw myself as being in the midst of a self-absorbing struggle, and I had all too little time for the feelings of others, and least of all for a Father who, encouraged by his friend the Head, had decided my future for me. Self-determination was in the air of the early 1960s – and in my reading of and about people like Kwame Nkrumah and Franz Fanon. Ridiculously, a little cloud settled over Nibley Farm and I could not see beyond it, and no one but me shared these problems, and if there were signs I should have read then I was too self-absorbed to read them. He went on hunting and he went on farming.

When we moved house I helped my mother with the packing, and my friend Harry Jupp came to stay to help us move boxes and pull nails out of the floors of Heath End Farm. The day we moved in was a hunt day, so of course no Father. My mother said he would have been a nuisance even if he had been there and we were better off without him. In truth, he had always been a dedicated follower of his pleasures and now we let him get on with it. Only piecemeal and over the next few years was I accidentally to pick up the trail of his hurt and his sense of betrayal.

This is where the years of arm's-length stand-off began. As we have seen, Father had never been an engaged parent. Now he distanced himself completely. Moreton friends reported back: "Your old man says you got so brainy and high fly-in' now, you don't speak to the likes of him!"

These and other jibes went deep.

"Your old man said you were too clever by half to dirty your hands with man's work."

This went particularly deep, since it followed the popular farming line that the only real work was done with your hands, that my mother's brothers were "clever pen pushers" and (here I hear a chorus of farm workers shouting approval) "no one not working on a farm knew what it was to do a proper day's work."

I knew Father did not really believe these things and I knew he would never say them directly to me. They made me angry at the time, since the last thing I wanted to do was to cut myself off from the countrymen amongst whom I had grown up. And then I felt sad when I heard him say to strangers, time and again, but always in my hearing, or voice raised so I would hear it:

"Oh, Dave? No, he was far too clever to come farming. He does something up in town ... No, I'm not sure what but I expect he'll get a good deal of money by it ... Farming's just about over of course ... He left us behind here to scratch in the dirt ... It's a humble living but all I can do..."

Father's impressions of Uriah Heep made the whole family squirm. What could he be thinking about as he portrayed himself as a poor old man bereft of a son and heir, left to meander on in lonely agricultural pursuits until finally snuffed out by age and infirmity? Apart from self-pity, with which we were both richly endowed, I know that he really missed my companionship. From 1963 until the early 1970s he schooled himself to show no public interest in me: if I had decided to go my own way then that was my business. I was no longer a factor in his life. Of course that broke down a few times when he did need help, but he was pretty consistent until we began to grow back towards each other in the next decade. He belonged, by age, century and gender, to a social category never able to speak easily about their emotions. While he could play the victim very well, his upbringing, the loss of his father and the very husbandry that he practiced had cauterised him securely against emotional pain. He behaved as if nothing moved him. But I knew it did.

There is another aspect to this as well. I longed for the gift of his approval. By excluding my life as an independent person, almost my existence, from his conversation and apparent interests through these years he denied me that approval. I knew it was a punishment. Later, when it didn't matter, he was generous in praising my achievements, but this proved impossible for him at the time. Looking back, I wonder if, as well as everything else concerning family and farming and succession, he may also have felt envy. I had exercised choices that he felt he had never been permitted, even if in fact he would never have taken them. I sensed that he felt that I had "got away with it", and he had not.

Did I feel the pain of a rupture between the two of us? I certainly knew that something was not right, though it was easy not to dwell upon it. In these years I scrambled for the requisite qualifications, got my place at Cambridge, enjoyed a life-changing three years, found a job, got married and had a first child. I worried about Father, but pretended that he really wasn't my problem. But the emotion I felt most was guilt. When I reached university the anger at the unreasonableness of a world that would not let me decide my own direction slackened off. The guilt remained. Guilt at not honouring the letter of the headmaster's agreement and not returning to farming at the end of that year. Guilt at running off to London to get my qualifications and do my university entrance in defiance of his known wishes. Guilt above all for not being the son he wanted and expected. Years later, when this period was well and truly over, he would tell the world of his pride in me, and that assuaged some of the guilt. My pride in knowing one of the last of the yeoman hunting farmers through his many eccentricities is one of the reasons for this book.

Did he feel that he had "lost" in the struggle between us about my future? My belief is that he did. I also thought that he blamed my mother for aiding and abetting the escape. If he did, and I certainly recall the comments to the effect that she always took my side, then he may have reflected on the irony here. In undertaking to bend himself to farming disciplines for a lifetime, his mother and mine gave him his hunting. I see us now as both driven in the same way towards those elements of life that were the foundation of contentment, in his case hunting, in mine a love of study and scholarship, and both of us struggling fiercely to obtain them. It would have made a great difference if either of us could have discussed any of this at all with the other.

Why was I so slow to realise this, I wonder now? Gloucester-shire County Council are partly to blame. In their decency they awarded me a full means-tested scholarship when I won a university place. When I compare this to the burden of educational debt borne by my own children I am amazed and grateful, and aghast at the way in which our accountant was able to produce the right number of years of farming losses to justify the award in full. Yet, generous as it was, it left a gap, the ten-week summer break, and a problem, in that I was too proud to ask for an allowance. I always knew that I would be generously fed and watered at home, and that my mother would give me money whenever asked and without hesitation. But I could not bear the thought of him saying, or even thinking "shirks the honest toil of the fields, yet still has to be supported with (a favourite phrase) unearned subventions." There was only one answer, and it has been obvious to students through the ages: get a job, earn enough to bridge the summer and get a little reserve for the coming year.

This practice began in the year of my involuntary exit from school. Once I had moved to London my growing sense of independence from Father and his wishes and expectations blossomed and bloomed. While I studied Latin at night, I found a girlfriend learning Italian from Tullio de Vecchi, our mutual tutor. She had lost a leg in a childhood accident, and I came to love her courage and her intellectual curiosity and her blazing honesty. Through her I met her family, emigré Austrian Jews, and her wonderful Oma, who had spent a lifetime fleeing persecution – from the Black Hundreds in her Polish Galician birthplace, to the fascism of Admiral Horthy's Hungary, to the Anschluss and Hitler in Austria. She was adding delightfully accented English to these as her fifth language.

My struggles seemed Lilliputian compared to the disasters these people had overcome, and they generously took on an untutored farmer's boy. From schnitzel to strudel, I loved their food. My girlfriend's father, a famous sportswear manufacturer, kept me in clothes, and Uncle Zoltan opened a Marxist door in my head which admitted György Lukács and Antonio Gramsci. By the end of my London year my political stance was wholly different from anything encountered in Cotswold life. I was already unrecognisable to myself from the school leaver of the previous year when I set off for a working summer in the Hotel St Cergue in the Swiss Canton de Vaud near Nyon. My duties included porter, laundryman, kitchen hand, washer-up and assistant to Monsieur le Golf and Monsieur le Tennis. I was rolling the courts when I received a telegram from my mother. I had passed my Latin! The last barrier was down. My place at Cambridge was confirmed. I felt I was free. But sadly, I did not feel like reconciliation. Instead I was impelled by the feeling of needing to distance myself from the world of the farm.

So I stayed away during those long, hot summers of the early 1960s. I persuaded myself, with some justice, that this was all part of my education, and a necessary rectification to the unrealities of life in a small Cotswold village. Sheffield became an early focus, and working in the steel mills of Steel, Peech and Tozer at Templeborough on the Rotherham Road, or the Batchelors Pea cannery in Hillsborough, persuaded me that all growing up was not as I had experienced it.

Drinking on Attercliffe Common and working night shifts or 4 a.m. shift starts from digs in the Ecclesall Road deepened and intensified my socialism and my sense of wanting to put feudal Gloucestershire behind me. The same feeling drove me to a working summer in the Whitbread hopfields of the Weald of Kent, making friends in West Ham and Barking that lasted for years, then down to Cardiff, where I eventually became a shepherd at Sully hospital, on the road to Barry Island where my sheep not only grazed the hospital parkland of this former TB hospital, but also supplied subjects for experimental heart valve operations.

In my breaks, my socialism took further flight as I sat on a bench beside Stan Awbery, dying TB victim and former Bristol MP for twenty years, as he described socialism and the Independent Labour Party in the valleys before the First World War. He gave me his local history book *I Searched for Llantwit Major*, and I stuffed it into the pocket of the Wimpey donkey jacket that I wore then with insufferable, unearned proletarian pride. I lost the jacket, but by great good fortune I still have the book.

The next job was at Truslove and Hanson, an upmarket bookshop in Knightsbridge. The work was not difficult even if the well-bred ladies who popped across the road from Harrods were ("I need romance with a touch of mystery, but not too steamy. What does your mother read?")

The young women assistants in the staff cubbyhole give me one-line summaries of the latest bodice rippers and I sell as confidently as I judged pigs. But I stay in London: held by love and Bayswater life and a new job, writing book reviews at £5 each for William Miller and John Boothe at the infant Panther paperback publishing house, the results to be typed by my girlfriend and then read to William in the Sun & 13 Cantons in Soho.

"No literary merit at all? Then that's for John's pile. But I am so pleased you liked the Violette Leduc. It might be impenetrable in parts but it is so of its day!"

Three years at Cambridge flew by, and if I wasn't there or working, my idea of a holiday took me hitch-hiking across Europe. Sitting on the pavement in the hot dust outside of the door of Salamanca's old cathedral one day a kindly soul, seeing the need for alms, released a stream of small coins into the cap that I had just removed from my head. While I later injected this hoard into the poor box where it properly belonged, I felt a curious satisfaction, a sense of being favoured by fate. Here I was taking my place as a European, away from tedious, vicious, insular English nationalism, recognised as just such another man in the street, no better or worse than my fellows, but carrying no special obligations to anyone for anything. It was a good feeling, but it was of course a lie. I had huge obligations and much to be grateful about, and even if I could not be a farmer I needed to be a family member, and a useful one as well. If I had struggled successfully to assert my right to determine how I would spend my life, my very success in achieving that independence meant that I should be giving back more, not less. In the Jewish tradition that I was joining, I learnt that sadness and pride can accompany a son growing up and overtaking his father.

How long it took me to realise this, to move beyond the thought to appropriate action, is a matter of shame, and much of that shame only came to light for me in a two-year period of twice-weekly psychotherapy in the mid 1980s. Then I realised what dangers we had both avoided. But when I left university in 1967 I was quite unaware. I had carefully repressed the bitterness and hurt I had felt at being told that I was not the son I ought to have been, the heir to generations of Cotswold farmers. Father now said nothing about what he felt. He came to Cambridge once but never again. He reported that the countryside was as interesting as "looking at the backside of a saucer" and he didn't know if he wanted to endure that again. His decision not to come to my graduation caused my mother great heartache, especially when her brother Don was outraged and showed up in their stead.

And if they had come, what could I have told them? My Cambridge life, beyond the university library and my trundling efforts on the rugby field would have been profoundly disturbing. My mother's politics were proto-Thatcherite before that lady came on stage. Would either of them have been impressed by the co-editor of *Cambridge Forward*, the university Labour Club magazine? Or the ward organiser for Trumpington ward in the 1964 and 1966 general elections? Or the co-organiser of the joint Oxbridge March on 4 June 1965 on Eton College itself to demand action on Labour's manifesto promise on the removal of charitable tax status from public schools, whose abolition we believed was the only way to secure lasting change in our country? It seemed at the time wiser not to parade these things as achievements, or indeed later activity as a part-time constituency agent for Labour in King's Cross and then Battersea South.

Not being there meant not being tempted into argument or disclosure, but not being there was also unsustainable. I owed my mother too much. She wanted to see me and whatever the difficulties with Father I had to go. These meetings could be stressful, guarded even, but they were necessary. I did not believe in the "not on speaking terms" conventions so much in use in families of my parent's generation, but I had to admit that Father and I, polite and circumspect as we were in company, were almost at that point.

Then one day, while I was visiting, John and Elsie Hodge dropped by. John was a local farm manager, a man from a non-agricultural background who had fought to get into the business. Tragically, a rare disease was quickly taking his eyesight and he was expecting to be blind in the next few months. His wife Elsie was vivacious, outspoken, tactless and childless. They had been kind when we arrived at Heath End Farm and despite a difference of twenty years between them and my parents, they became good friends.

I absented myself from a convivial tea party, but was in the kitchen when Elsie came in to top up the teapot. She walked straight up to me and said:

"David, you must do something for your father."

When I did not respond she said: "John said that with his eyes going he could just do with a son on the farm. Your father said that if he had the choice of a son or his eyesight, he would take the eyesight!"

I do not recall where the rest of that conversation went. I was reeling from the remark which felt like a knife thrust into my carefully buried hurt. Did my father really feel that deeply? He had never shown it. His attitude now seemed to me to be one of acceptance of what I saw as an event in the recent past, but obviously I could not tell. The fact that I did not know how Father actually felt about not having a farmer as a son, as well as what this meant for the future of the farm, was now obvious.

I had a further reminder, just as sharp in its way, a few months later. As I drove into the yard I saw Charm Fleming, our neighbour from Turkdean, leaning against her car. I parked and walked back to her. She had brought her butler, Regent, over to see Father with a large box of spare pieces of "tack" from her stables, and they were now busily engaged in rummaging in Father's similar resources to find Pelhams and bits, or girths and leading reins, that matched up with stuff they already had to make complete sets. The chatelaine of Leygore was as regular as Father in her hunting pursuits with the Heythrop. I knew he held her in high regard, loved her tart commentary on other hunting folk and her sly sense of humour. She said she had gone down to the house to see my mother but found she was out. I was just about to offer drinks and other refreshments when I caught an intense stare and stopped.

"You will never know, thank goodness, what pain and heart-ache you have caused your father. You can't help it, I know. Same thing with us, I tell him. One in each generation has to be sacrificed to banking. But, David, he has no one else…he can't just throw a cousin or a nephew into the works. You really must see how he feels about it even if, as I fully understand, you can do nothing now to change anything."

And then, and I wish her words were still in my mind, she started describing one of her family "who also felt that he had lost all connections to his son".

Was this how Father felt? Was this how he described our relationship to his friends? My head filled with possible replies. Did she realise that Heath End Farm was not an hereditary property? That I was settled in London as a young publisher, and expecting a family? Father talking to her about his loss now was resurrecting history with a vengeance. Or did he just confide his sense of loss and disappointment to these women to excite interest and sympathy?

As usual I did not know what to say, so I offered a glass of sherry and we went into the farmhouse. My mother soon re-appeared, but even after our visitor departed, I could not tell her what had happened. At this point in their long and sustaining relationship she would have told him, probably in quite forceful terms, that if he had any disappointments in life he could tell her or otherwise keep them to himself. So what could I do? Broach the subject direct? Have it out and clear the air? My wife felt that this was the best course, but what she did not know, because I had never told her, was that I had only ever had one full and frank discussion with Father since the day when I walked away from the meeting with him and the headmaster, triumphant at having won an extra year at school.

The discussion had happened four years later when I had just left Cambridge and was living with my girlfriend and her family in London. I had told my mother on the phone that I had proposed to Vienne and that we were going to get married.

When I next arrived at the farm my mother greeted me.

"Your father needs to speak to you about something impor-tant – alone," she said and disappeared into the kitchen. I went into the sitting room and there he was, standing awkwardly in front of the fireplace, fidgeting from foot to foot as if he were standing amongst the coals themselves.

I greeted him but he did not respond to the greeting but burst into a preprepared speech that came out all in a rush.

"Now, Dave, this idea of a marriage. Your mother and I have discussed it. We must ask ... no, we must advise you ... well, we say anyway that what you have got to do is put this out of your mind for a few years. Just forget it, that's what we say. Please do that for us. We cannot bear to see you throwing away your life and all chances of happiness."

There was a pause. Then I choked out,

"Why? It's *my* life! What can you possibly object to?"

The answer was very well-rehearsed.

"Well, three things. You are far too young for a start, as well as being unemployed. And then, she is handicapped, an amputee. We cannot see that such a marriage could possibly last. You will get tired of the limitations it will impose after a few years, and how can she possibly have children? And we know nothing about her people. They are Jews and Austrians and while they may be decent people, for all we know, their customs and standards will be different. We think it will be impossible to form a relationship with them – we simply won't be able to understand them."

Another pause. Then I found myself saying, more brusquely than I meant,

"Well, thanks for the advice. But I am over 21 and require no permission from anyone. I am older than my sister when you gave her permission to get married. I came to tell you today that I now have a job in publishing in London, starting in October at £850 per annum, and since she works as well we should be self-supporting when we marry next year. We are assured that we can have children and intend to do so. And I am planning to bring the whole family of future in-laws down from London in two weeks' time. They too are worried that your rural accents will be so thick that they will not understand your English!"

Father did not say another word on the subject until after the wedding was over. Then I took him with my mother back to Paddington, and while she found them seats on the Moreton-in-Marsh train, he leaned morosely out of the carriage window.

"Well, that's it then. I shall never visit London again. Nothing happens here which will ever be of interest to me!"

And in one sense he was quite right: in all the years that I lived there he never came on a visit again or entered a house that I owned. But in every other sense he was quite wrong. Those two families did get on very well. Both my parents loved Oma, Father enjoyed smoking Austrian cheroots with Uncle Zoltan and was only slightly abashed when my father-in-law asked how many golf courses could be carved out of the farm. As time went on my wife became one of my mother's protégées, and my mother was deeply influential in her life, a universal source of best practice on all matters culinary and childcare, a relationship that endured beyond the twenty years of the marriage itself. And if that element of Father's prognostication did at length come true, though for other reasons, something happened in the meanwhile that brought Father and me back together in a shared context where the events of the past simply did not intrude.

When I think of it I see two men struggling with the head of a small but very pretty pony. It takes one of us on either side to guide Rocky in any given direction. The rider, small and vociferous and making all the necessary movements with reins and knees and crop to obtain forward impulsion, is my very frustrated daughter Kate. She wants Rocky to go down the lane past the donkeys in the next field. Rocky cannot abide donkeys and sees no need for exercise. He has learnt that if you are stubborn enough folk will let you do what you want.

I look across at Father, concentrating on keeping the precious cargo in the saddle with one hand while trying to pull the reluctant steed forward with the other. This is the man who did not buy ponies for children. This is the man who spent little time with his own children. This is an infatuated grandfather.

Now there is time, and my mother is similarly infatuated. My wife finds the farm terrain difficult, but is mostly concerned that Kate will be bored in a London flat alone. She is therefore literally "farmed out" in the holidays and is becoming more like another daughter. Father reads to her and she, in time, returns the favour. The old business between us is becoming less interesting now I am around more often because of Kate. Unlike the years before, during and after Cambridge I am not avoiding the farm but delighted to be there. Father and I are beginning to talk again. Are all of those years of difficulty and tough love to end not with a bang, but a whimper?

Now we were invested in a new generation. Both of us. The struggles of the previous generation seemed less important. But still we had no common ground, no shared pursuit, nothing in common. All we really needed now was something to do while getting down to the business of rediscovering each other.

Chapter 24

Relationships Redeemed

I T CAME IN A BOX. Somehow this made it seem more formal than when I had first seen it. Then it was just a jumble of mallets and balls and hoops. Like so much of the accoutrements of Father's life, it came by accident. We had visited a country house sale a month or so earlier, Father as ever prowling the stables for job lots of saddlery, or some unused horseshoes.

He was in luck, there were two such lots. One of them had the croquet set which had occupied the pre-1914 house parties who had enjoyed those lawns. He turned to me and asked which one he should bid for in the auction. By great good fortune I opted for the croquet. The lawns at Evenlode ran right around three sides of the house, and while they were a bit uneven in places and generally sloped down towards the fields, surely we could fit in a croquet pitch?

We were the only bidders. I gave our address to the auctioneer for the delivery and we went our way. I was in my late twenties, with Cambridge five years behind me. Father had now been at Evenlode for eight years. I was married, as we have seen, with an infant daughter to whom both my parents were devoted. I had a job in the London office of Thomas Nelson and Sons, a Scottish educational publisher acquired by the Thomson Corporation from Canada. I found a passion for producing school textbooks and sought ways of making them more effective as a means of knowledge transfer and communication. In other words, I had settled into a new life and was a bit pompous about it.

Much the same could be said of Father. He had left behind him at Nibley Farm all of the struggle for survival and fear of failure that had dogged him since his earliest farming days. His children had all grown up, left home and were self-supporting. He had a mortgage that was serviceable without the twice-daily sweat labour of the milking parlour. He still had some land at Nibley which might be needed for housing or industrial use, and meanwhile provided security. On the work of one man and himself, Heath End Farm, Evenlode was a manageable and mostly arable farming unit with good grazing land in the water meadows alongside the Evenlode river. If life was becoming easier, his temperament was changing too, as he slowly became the benign and ever-amusing and whimsical grandfather that his grandchildren remember.

None of this was achieved in a hurry. There were still times when the gambling man in Father emerged, still times when the eccentricity had fermented to a point where the cork had to be eased to release pressure in the bottle. In the latter category, elderly residents of Evenlode village looked askance at his habit of exercising horses on dark winter evenings, and when the ghost rider tapped with his whip on a lighted upstairs window one night as he passed, he was fortunate that the the petrified widow who had been soaking in her bath tub was a friend of my mother and at length forgave him. He was becoming the sort of person from whom this sort of behaviour might be expected, and as always he played outrageously to any audience he could gather.

In the gambling category lies the episode of the Welsh ewes. It reminded me of nothing so much as the time when, twenty years earlier, we had been sold down a river of Savoy cabbages. One similarity in both stories had been the tipster – the man who gave Father the nod and the wink which "put him on" to a certain winner that no one else had noticed. All that needed to be done was to invest heavily, distorting all other activities to make the miracle work, cash in and then be recognised as the genius agriculturalist which Father knew, and should Providence allow, he really was.

Tom Williams, a charismatic vegetable wholesaler in Bristol, worked the Savoy cabbage charm. He saw our Mill and Pike ground at Nibley as ideal for a winter crop of the aptly named variety Winter King. What could be better – a late winter cash crop, bringing revenues at a time when they were most needed. Father planted the field in an excess of excitement. They flourished and grew and his passion for this cash-flow solution grew with them.

Then came the day when Tom Williams arrived with a truck load of nets. He patiently explained that each net would be filled with 28 cabbages. Each cabbage must be trimmed of its outer leaves since these could not be sold. Cabbages could only be cut in the mornings or they would dry out and reduce the weight. He would phone us every evening to tell us how many nets he needed for the following day, and would collect promptly at 6.30 a.m. for the Bristol wholesale market. Please do not make the drivers wait, were his parting words, or you will miss the best prices.

There was an uncomfortable silence after he left. It was clear that no part of the logistics of this deal had for a moment entered Father's head. But family must cope, and my sister Jane, recently returned from Hartbury Agricultural College, led the charge. Next morning, at 5.30, we had knives and were hard at it, wet to the skin as the Savoys emptied rain and dew in bucket loads as we cut and trimmed. Triumphant the first day, we were heartily sick of winter cabbage by the end of the month, but our brassica blues did not prevent him from doing the same with Brussels sprouts the following year. After all, he was milking while all of this went on, and when he emerged we seemed to have finished. And still only 7.30, in time for a day's work, or school!

So we were filled with foreboding when the man from Brecon Beacons to whom Father sold our wonderful May hay, full of Timothy and meadow fescues, a pure delight to horses, remarked that the thing to be doing now was Welsh ewes. People today had smaller families and were eating less meat. They wanted smaller joints, and on our rich land the hardy Welsh sheep, bred for moorland and mountain, would put on condition very quickly. They were cheap to buy just then. Father needed no second invitation.

Within weeks he was at the Craven Arms sales in Shropshire, eager to buy and get started. He told us he might buy fifty to try: he came home with a hundred and fifty. "They were just too cheap." And they looked wonderful in our home fields, far more ornamental than the small flock of Jacobs we had once tried. Father contacted a neighbour in Kitebrook, and he brought along his Border Leicester ram. We loaded the marker on a harness around his belly and soon had visual evidence of his energy and prowess. Father crowed that night and, the weekend over, I returned to London.

That Thursday I had a call from my mother. Father had been up several times in the night since the ram had finished his work and gone home. We had callers from as far away as Dorn and Longborough reporting our sheep for straying, and eating their crops. The little sheep slipped through our hedges so easily that we could not keep them in. The plan now was to line the hedges in the home fields with wire mesh, but help was needed to put in posts and nail it up. The task took a full two days, but when finished we had two secure fields. I left Father with the problem of what to feed them once they had close grazed their new home: he solved the problem by buying in hay and they thus ate his profit margin. This, it emerged, was the least of our problems. Winter's advance meant the grass was diminishing anyway. Time to bring them under cover and await lambing.

Our cover was something we had not really considered. We had a disused cowshed at Evenlode as well as a (full) Dutch barn, but no cover for a hundred and fifty sheep. What the heck! These are hardy mountain beasts. Let them stay in the fields and if any of them need lambing assistance we would administer it where they lay. They were used to lambing in the open on Snowdonia. No problem. I took a fortnight's holiday at Christmas and was glad I did. When I arrived two problems had already emerged. Welsh ewes bearing small Welsh lambs were one thing: bearing larger Leicester lambs was quite different. Every mother was in difficulty, every ewe needed help. Unfortunately no one had told them that Father and I were the only available help.

On our approach they got up and started to run. To my amazement, even a ewe half through labour could move at high speed and then would be difficult to spot in the snow. Did I forget to say that it began to snow the day after I arrived? It drifted deeply in front of those wire mesh fences. By the third day about half of the sheep were invisible, but at least the snow slowed them down a little.

Father and I took it in turns on the two routines we developed. One would rescue ewes in trouble and load them into the Land Rover. Once we had two we would drive back to the cowshed where the other had a trestle table to put the sheep on while we worked on delivery issues. We then had a warm straw-lined pen for them and if necessary milk for a struggling lamb.

Often delivery problems could be solved quickly and easily by getting our hands on the big lambs' front legs and easing them out. Sometimes the previous efforts had so exhausted the ewe that we lost her. Rarely, we had a lamb positioned the wrong way round in the womb and this was usually fatal, since the lambs were too big to turn round. And we lost some ewes and lambs in the drifts where we had failed to find them.

The cowshed at night looked like a particularly manic set for *M*A*S*H* during a North Korean advance. Mercifully for the weary staff it only lasted four days and nights but the casualty rate was appalling. Twenty-eight ewes and seventeen lambs were lost. There were no living twin lambs. This was the last of Father's great adventures. After this we settled for as much boring normality as we could get, without sheep of any type at all.

And we still had croquet. When the box was delivered it was left in the barn and the following summer some impulse persuaded us to open it up and have a look. It was immaculate. Mallets and hoops, multi-coloured stripped poles for start and finish. There was even a special mallet for hammering in the hoops. There were six balls of different colours, and two books of rules, governing Association, Lawn and Golf Croquet. Father gave them to me, bidding me learn them and teach him. Meanwhile he took the plan and said he would lay out the pitch in time for my next visit.

When that day came I realised I had fallen short. I had left the rules in the car and had never looked at them. But neither had Father laid out the pitch. He soon explained why. Extensive as his lawns were, and close mown as they were by Father on a huge sit-on motor mower, there was no space that exactly fitted the dimensions of the required rectangle. Even if we scaled it down a bit the only space was on the side lawn, which sloped down to the ha-ha where I had done my final practice work as a builder of drystone walls. Would the slope distort the true course of the ball when struck with a mallet? Rather like Minehead golf course, everything we did on that slope rolled gracefully across the sward ... until, on slowing, it turned sharply to the edge and plunged over the lip of the lawn and down into the ditch of the ha-ha beneath it. That deep ditch was wet and putrid, even in a dry summer, and we soon tired of climbing the stile from the garden into the field beyond to get the ball back from the ha-ha ditch. The ha-ha was wonderful at preventing cows and horses from climbing up onto the lawn. It was wonderful at providing people in the house or on the lawn with a view of the surrounding countryside uncluttered by intervening fences. It was not built to stop croquet balls in any circumstances.

So it was clear we had to think again. Father poured his gin and perry concoction, source and origin of so many strange ideas, and we considered what we might do to croquet, or something like it, in the extensive space available. After tea the answer emerged. Mini golf croquet. We hammered in the start and finish posts on either side of the farmhouse and ranged the hoops so that our course framed the house in a U shape. The distance between hoops could be up to sixty feet. You were to start at one striped post and then go all around the house to the other, and then turn there for the return journey. First home was the winner. If you encountered the ball of your opponent, then you were allowed to place your ball next to his and strike both in a way which allowed you to progress round the course but sent him spinning away to destruction (or the ha-ha), thus reducing his chances of getting home first. And after these collisions, which we dutifully and correctly called a "roquet", the successful player got a free go. So useful when your opponent was in front of a hoop and about to go through: you could creep up, touch him, go through while pushing him to hell in a handcart, to use Father's expression, and then get off towards the next hoop while leaving him to trudge back to navigate the previous one.

We played our first game that evening, found the slopes difficult in the half light, and the bias of the ball hard to predict.

I was surprised when Father asked if I fancied a game after breakfast, but played along. By lunchtime we were compulsive gamblers, demanding the next game as a way of mitigating the losses of the last round. By teatime we were locked in trench warfare, each with their hands around each other's throats, unable to release our grip. By dinner time, to my mother's astonishment we were telling anecdotes of the outrageous shots, the skill and the luck of the other and the brilliance and mastery which we ourselves had displayed.

Whatever had happened in the past now became part of the history of other people. It was as if we had found a place where being a father or a son was not really so important after all.

Did it really matter who succeeded whom at what? What did matter was getting the cutter bar on the mower so low that the grass was almost shiny, sending the ball skidding from the mallet, making knowledge of slope and roll and weight of strike vital to success. We had found what we did together, and thus, as we did it, we could talk of things that we had never talked about before. We had found out how companionship works, and it never subsequently departed over the next twenty or so years. We were joined by a trivial pursuit, but once joined, it enabled everything else to be said.

In the months and years that followed this sense of enjoyment in each other's company never left us. Whether sitting in the Fox at Evenlode or its namesake at Broadwell over a pint of sludgy Longborough Ales, or slowly meandering country lanes in the Land Rover, commentating over passing hedges on the sins of commission or omission of other farmers, we found a relationship neither filial nor paternal. He took to writing, often two or three times a week. I took to buying books, first of all to satisfy "I always wished I'd read that, Dave" statements, and then because I really wanted to see if he too loved things that I had loved. It was not that either of us changed our lives in any marked manner. He was still the passionate hunting farmer, with the lawn meet of the Heythrop at the farm on his birthday each year as the centrepiece of his dedication. He became in his seventies less active as a farmer, outsourcing cultivations to local contractors, and while he had little time for organised religion or politics, he loved to talk, wisely and well, with a croquet mallet in his hand.

"I think I can be reasonably proud of that shot," begins one of those letters as he expostulated against the complacent self-satisfaction of his brother-in-law. Though I had a great deal to be grateful for concerning my mother's brother, Father was hugely irritated, especially when Don, a seasoned golfer, visited and got the hang of the croquet course after a few days. Father's spirit, as in the hunting field, was still competitive. His joy at roqueting an opponent and sending them skidding into the ha-ha was the same, if it was a lusty adult guest only playing to humour him or a small child playing for the first time.

"Not worth playing if you don't want to win."

He frowned on my tendency to handicap, giving extra shots to the halt or the sick.

"No mollycoddling!"

Games were a serious part of life. Had he not always demonstrated this through his pursuit of fox and hounds?

Chapter 25

Father Argonautica

W E DISCUSSED IT in the car going down to Bristol. My mother had decided, as Father entered his seventies, that I should accompany him and, in time, drive him to meetings with lawyers and real estate agents in Bristol. Our lawyers were Burges Salmon, where my mother had once worked and who were still one of the leading agricultural law firms in the country. Our advisers on land sales were Alder King, where Cousin Richard was a senior partner. We still had a few pieces of land at Nibley Farm. Yate, the nearest town, had been designated as an over-spill housing area beyond the Bristol green belt. Employment came from two engineering works in the town, and there was a demand for warehousing as major truck routes were diverted to avoid the city of Bristol and go round it on the motorway network. We had a piece of land that would make an excellent business park and warehouse site, and if we succeeded in developing it then the farm at Evenlode would become clear of mortgages and entailments. Father remarked that most of his family "died with their debts." He wanted to be an exception.

The journey down to Bristol always took at least two hours. Father did not want to drive, to my huge relief, but was carsick when driven. Dosed by my mother with Kwells, he took his seat beside me. I had a thermos of coffee and some fruit cake: stoppages were inevitable. Father felt that since the meeting centred on him and could not begin without him it did not matter much when we arrived. If they wanted to earn their fees they would wait. At this time I was chief executive of a small but innovative law publishing company, putting legal information on computer and making it searchable there. I had a pompous businessman's regard for the sanctity of meeting times being met.

As it happened we had something to discuss which made the journey go quicker. At an earlier meeting it became clear that the local authority and its planning committee had three different sites in mind. Naturally we thought ours the best. To clinch a deal and secure a "planning gain" for the planners it was suggested that we offer to build an access road on to our site and a roundabout to join it safely to the main road. This idea incensed Father.

"I farmed there for thirty years and that council never did a thing for me. They used to send inspectors to see how much my cows had soiled the roads, and letters ordering me to clear it up! Let them go hang. I'll burn in hell before I help one of those councillors across the road, let alone build a roundabout for them!"

With more in this vein, the journey went quickly. We did

not need to stop, though more Kwells were washed down with whisky from a concealed hip flask.

We were late. I made the apologies that Father avoided. He stumped into the conference room, drew two chairs out and placed them facing each other. He sat in one, placed his feet on the other and placed his hat over his face. After a pause, the slightly muffled voice from beneath the hat intoned,

"Let the boy speak for me. I want no more of it."

Indeed, it was clear from the commencement of heavy breathing that he had indeed left the meeting. The assembled company looked to me and, interrupted only by a few loud snores, we began the meeting. We were quickly able to agree a plan for the roundabout and alter our submission accordingly. In an hour we were through, and the senior partner's secretary was awakening Father with a cup of tea.

"All done?" he said.

"Well, I do hope you approve, Robert, since we have rather diverged from…"

"Diverged, be damned," said Father. "I said we would go with the boy and so we will. I would go with him anywhere."

I was overcome by this sudden flood of confidence in me. The planning application went in and eventually succeeded. But in the car going home I asked if he really meant what he said. Yes, he said, he certainly did. Then I told him about an idea I had been nursing.

"What if I said that I wanted, while you were still fit and well, to give you the opportunity to do something or go somewhere that you have wanted to do all your life and never been able to manage. I will plan it and fund it – just tell me what you want and trust me."

I anticipated that a reply might wait until I was next down from London, but it came immediately.

"Before I die, I must see those giant Irish foxhounds with a bit of wolfhound in their bloodline. Captain Wallace swore he had seen them grow to thirty inches to the shoulder but anything beyond twenty-eight would please me. And to breathe the air and walk the hills where they run."

Well, it seemed a simple request. I accepted the challenge of organising it immediately:

"Consider it done."

The following week in London I took a call from my mother:

"Your father tells me that you are taking him to Ireland."

I agreed that we were making a plan.

"Am I in your plan?"

I admitted that we had not quite got that far, only to be told that Father was a rotten traveller and did not enjoy moving around. She said that for her such a trip would be a punishment, and its objective was ludicrous: once you had seen one foxhound you had seen them all. On the other hand she would not let us go without responsible supervision. As much as Father's faith in my organisational powers had given me confidence this brought me back to ground level. She ended by saying that she would release Father into my custody so that I could take him to foreign places only if my sister Mary accompanied us.

"She is a great favourite with him and will be able to manage him when he goes stubborn and refuses to budge. You really haven't a clue about him. You will just shout and swear and he will do the same, so you need someone who really understands him."

This hurt. Post-reconciliation, I thought that my understanding had grown immensely. But if this was a condition of engagement then I had to accept in order to honour my promise.

All this came back into my mind, and in sharp focus, a few months later while sitting in the bar of Jury's hotel in Dublin.

I had met Father and Mary at the airport that morning. The two of them had checked in and gone to their rooms to freshen up. Mary had then joined me in the bar. We were having a drink and awaiting his arrival when the phone in the bar rang. The barman answered and then asked if I was Mr Worlock. I took the phone.

"For God's sake, will someone come and rescue me! Mary got me up here OK, but we are on the third floor and I can't find any stairs. Only this damned useless cage thing in the corridor. Like some blasted cattle crush. I shake the gates and can't seem to get in. Then it dashes off somewhere else before I can pry the gates open…"

And so, for the first time, we realised that he had never used a lift on his own. Mary dashed off to rescue him. I finished my drink in full realisation of my mother's concern.

The Irish trip had been facilitated by a very wonderful coincidence. At this time my company in London was engaged in a joint venture with the *Irish Times* newspaper. We were building an online service for Irish lawyers. I was in Dublin every month for board meetings and in social moments it was easy to ask advice on the location of the near-mythical beasts we sought and the travails we would have to overcome on the way to encountering them. The Irish, amongst all of their other many virtues, put filial piety in a special place. The chairman, the legendary Major Thomas Bleakey McDowell, the British army officer from Belfast who created the trust that still protects the independence of the newspaper, promised to make enquiries of his hunting friends.

Within days he was back with introductions: the two packs that sported such monsters were the Black and Tans (the Scarteen Hunt) and the Gallant Tipps (the Tipperary Foxhounds) and he had written a note of introduction to the masters of each, saying we would be in touch to arrange an appointment to measure and inspect the hounds in their kennels. He had also advised the master of the Galway Blazers (the County Galway Hunt) that we might be along since, when consulted, that eminence had told the chairman that the Black and Tans were "mere Kerry Beagles, dwarfed by the Blazers". The chairman, in his famous Bunker office in D'Olier Street, told me that avoiding disappointment was vital. He then said that the *Irish Times* would like to welcome "your old fellow" to Dublin with a private dinner. Would that be acceptable?

Consulted on hotels, Louis O'Neill, managing director at the newspaper, entered into the spirit of a journey which was now feeling less like Argonauts and more like minor royalty. Louis recommended castles and when our dates were available his secretary booked them, from Bunratty to Dromoland to Ashford to Ballynahinch. So we would not lack for good food and a comfortable bed.

Then Seamus Conaty, celebrated Cavan footballer, *The Times* of London executive, and now leading the digital charge at the *Irish Times*, landed the coup de grâce. Of all generous gestures, getting tickets for the grandstand at the Curragh and turning it into the opening of our journey, was inspired. When we had rescued Father from the third floor of the hotel we met Seamus at the front door and crowded into his car. We were, thanks to the extraordinary kindness of these people, off on our voyage.

The racing that day is lost in time, drowned out by the regular slugs of Jameson's between races. At one point I do recall Father wandering off and losing contact with us. Mindful of our mother's instructions that we had to bring him back alive and in one piece, we set up a hunt.

Mary stayed where she was while Seamus and I went in opposite directions to scour the bars, the betting facilities and the toilets. We met twenty minutes later on the top deck of the stand, next to the commentary box. No luck, we had drawn a blank. Then the door to the commentary box opened and Father emerged, shaking hands with the commentator.

"What a nice man," said Father. "We got talking about a horse and then he had to start the next race, so I had to stay with him until it was over."

"Do you know that man?" said Seamus.

"No," Father replied, "he was just standing there and he looked to me like someone I really should be speaking to… So I did."

"That was Michael O'Hehir, the most famous sports commentator in Ireland. Half the people in this stand would give their teeth for the opportunity you have just had!"

For a man with no social graces and little small talk except on horses and other livestock, Father found it remarkably easy to make social contact across all classes and conditions of mankind. Perhaps it was his artlessness, his innocence. He found it easy to be himself when he did not need, as when buying or selling, to pose or play a role. Even so, I found the approaching dinner with members of the *Irish Times* board rather worrying. Would he be relaxed, or feel he had to act up to some expectation that he imagined they might have? If he was nervous, might he drink too much? I determined to keep close to him so that I could intervene when conversations lapsed or grew difficult. I told myself I was being protective: in truth I was worried that he might disgrace himself and me too.

As soon as we sat down to dinner I let that cowardly thought slip and was ashamed of myself for even entertaining it. Father sat between the chairman and Louis O'Neill at the head of the table. No longer close, I strained to catch the conversation. All I got was gales of laughter. He loved them and it was mutual. The chairman barked his merriment down the table as he got off a good remark. Louis, normally shy and reserved, was grinning and twinkling.

I grew relaxed as the meal drew to a close. The chairman had been miffed because he could not get his favoured private room at the Kildare Street Club. He booked instead the upper room of the Lord Edward, then a French restaurant and not yet a seafood restaurant, between the castle and the cathedral. I had been asked what Father ate and incautiously answered "pheasant". Father complained that he could not read the French menu and Louis translated. Wine and waiters came and went. When only coffee and brandy remained, the chairman said words of warm welcome, to which Father properly and gratefully replied. Then Major Tom went off script:

"Now tell me, Robert," he said. "As a man of the country and a lover of pheasant, tell me if you enjoyed your dinner in one of the best French restaurants this city affords."

There was a brief silence, in which I mentally wrote and discarded two dozen replies to that question. Then Father responded.

"My dear wife, who I miss very much, would, were she here, stop me from answering that question. But you are my new-found friends. You have been so generous to me. In the absence of her restraint I can only respond with the truth … As I ate that pheasant, not hung, not roasted, covered in sauce, no port wine or redcurrant jelly in sight, I could conceive of how easily it might be confused with the corpse of a dead moggy, fished out of the middens of Dublin, basted in engine oil and served on a bed of decaying garden compost…"

Another silence which seemed to go on forever. Then an explosion of laughter from the chairman.

"Well, you will never make a politician or a newspaperman, that's for sure!"

The table seemed to glow (for months, visiting the newspaper or drinking in Bowes Tavern opposite it, journalists would smile at me and say "dead moggy" or ask me earnestly if he did say that). On the evening in question, what should have been a show stopper became a crowning glory. The most assiduous reteller of the tale was the chairman himself. And he started to tell the story by saying,

"When you ask someone to tell you the truth you don't always get what you expect."

As things so often do in Ireland, a little legend was born.

Later on, with Bowes Tavern friends from the newspaper sports desk, I had the pleasure of watching Barry McGuigan's Belfast fight prior to his successful world championship bid in London. They found me a seat in the press box, and amidst the post-fight camaraderie I was offered a seat in the BBC van going out to Aldersgrove airport in the morning. Here I was squashed in beside the veteran sports commentator, Harry Carpenter. When I introduced myself he said,

"I know about you. Aren't you the bloke whose father was given a dead cat for dinner in Dublin?"

Soon these urban myths and legends were behind us, however, as we drove out of Dublin in search of huge hounds. At first everything intrigued us and we travelled slowly. Men cutting peat in the Bog of Allen had to be closely questioned on cutting techniques and drying times. Walls made of huge topping stones and rounded basalt boulders had to be inspected. Farmers had to be stopped and questioned in the tradition of Arthur Young or William Cobbett. Back in the car, there was intensive discussion as we went further west on how agriculture could survive on the more marginal lands. Then as we climbed the Rock of Cashel and drank in the air once breathed by Brian Boru, we looked out on a vista of Ireland unified as an island fifty years before the

Conqueror set foot on Pevensey Bay. After Cashel we became more attuned to the pace and tone of the western counties. After a long and slothful drive one day, our landlord, discovering that we were devoted to the horse, assumed that we had come for the monthly sales.

"I'll make sure you are up by six and get a good breakfast," he said. "They start at seven sharp and all the best beasts are gone by ten!"

The sales took place at a moorland crossroads some fifteen miles away. By the time we arrived the place was crowded, with cars and horseboxes pulled on to every grass verge. I dropped my passengers at the Cross and found a parking space half a mile away. By the time I returned, Father was already surrounded by dealers like mosquitoes in an equatorial jungle. Fights threatened to break out as they competed for the attentions of the find of the day – a gullible Englishman with more money than sense who would surely want to take home a pleasant hacking cob, quiet in company? Or this wonderful chestnut mare, good with hounds, property of a lady who had a hip replacement and can't hunt? Or perhaps a delightful Connemara pony for the grandchildren when they come to stay, very tolerant with the young, well-mannered, perfect for gymkhanas?

"Oh, sir, can you not picture the little ones winning the musical chairs on that one?"

"Oh, sir, of course you are not too heavy for the mare. She could carry you all day, and Brian Boru himself on the back for ballast."

"Oh, sir, that's not a cough. Just clearing his throat. Why, we take such care of him we even steam his hay!"

Similar knots of petitioners and potential buyers have formed at various places on the roads around the Cross. Horses are being trotted to and fro in front of appraising eyes. No market rules here, and no auctioneers either. It is a world of cash and *caveat emptor*. The landlord is right. By ten the crowds are clearing. We realise that since we arrived no traffic has used the crossroads, but now cars are beginning to nudge through the thinning crowds. A few last, determined sellers, who gave up hope of us earlier, now return, but depart frustrated. The mist has lifted from the moor and it is time to go.

The Open Road is becoming our great resource. We do not plan. We steer only by the dog hounds. The Gallant Tipps are not quite big enough to be wholly satisfying, so we head north-west, but not before a night in a Limerick bar ends with a mass effort to teach Father the words to "The Fields of Athenry". Once he realizes this is a convict song from the famine years, he wipes away a tear.

"The terrible things we have done to Ireland." His emotions are as close to the surface as any Irishman.

Soon we all cry together, and then sing "Danny Boy", and then we all cry again. I see that in one sense the trip is tiring Father: he is not used to having his emotions washed in public. He is called upon for empathy and sympathy more often in a day than in a month in the Cotswolds. Now every beggar, every broken down donkey, every lame dog pausing before a stile, calls out to him. But in Galway we find hounds big enough to satisfy innumerable Jasons and a boatload of Argonauts. They recall to Father the hound puppies he has trained in the past: Reason and Rosary, Wisecrack and Wildrose, Parallel and Partial. Prize winners all at the Beaufort and the Heythrop puppy shows, he tells the kennel huntsman. He has the silverware to prove it. They are impressed. And so is he.

He recalls the puppies we walked, now fully grown hounds at his lawn meet; recognising and cornering my daughter, putting their paws on her shoulders and licking her helpless face.

"If we had walked puppies here she could have ridden them home when her feet got tired."

As we leave the emotions are bubbling again. He grasps us both and mutters something about dreams coming true and his deep gratitude. And then,

"I have found so much here that I never imagined I could ever encounter…"

Ireland has not done with him yet, however. As a sixth former I had become addicted to the poetry of William Butler Yeats. So much of the majesty and mystery of what Father is experiencing is there. I have brought my school prize, my *Collected Yeats*, with me and persecute my fellow travellers when they are trying to rest. Now I beg them to go further north with me, to see Thoor Ballylee at Gort, where the poet wrote, and Lady Gregory's now empty Coole Park.

He is not impressed by the tower, which he thinks dark and gloomy, and the park, its house now demolished, has to be an exercise in imagination:

> Great rooms where travelled men and children found
> Content or joy; a last inheritor
> Where none has reigned that lacked a name and fame
> Or out of folly into folly came.

Their imaginations were working overtime and I was trying hard to recapture the voice from the scratchy old Caedmon record of 1931 from which I first heard the poet read. We rounded a corner and there was the lake. I tried again, with Yeats's swans taking off from its still waters:

> Another emblem there! That stormy white
> But seems a concentration of the sky;
> And, like the soul, it sails into the sight
> And in the morning's gone, no man knows why;
> And is so lovely that it sets to right

What knowledge or its lack had set awry,
So arrogantly pure, a child might think
It can be murdered with a spot of ink.

I spare them the poet's gloomy conclusions: we are on holiday. But I think they feel for the mystery of things in this place of visions and poets and writers, and in the next moment we have Father at the Autograph Tree, deciphering the names of her ladyship's distinguished guests cut into its bark.

Here is Yeats himself, and AE, Sean O'Casey and J. M. Synge. Here is George Bernard Shaw and at least one Irish President, Douglas Hyde. Suddenly he sees it: like the fashionable house parties at Badminton or Lyegrove, viewed from afar in his youth, a literary salon and a great flowering of Irish writing.

But now he is restless for more countryside. We drive down to the Burren country, that great stone yard in County Clare. Now he complains that there is too much rock. He needs to see farming. We are unmoved. We want to see dolmen and a hermit's cave, and prehistoric sites with the remains of bears.

This last, encountered near the great Cliffs of Moher, is at the end of a three-mile path down to the base of the cliff through rock tunnels. The rain is falling, emptying the Atlantic back on top of us, but it will be dry inside. The car park is on a a steep slope above the legendary cliffs and we find a place in the front row, overlooking the sea.

So, Father, are you coming? No, he is not. If he wants to see a bear he can go to the zoo. It's raining. He is an old man. You kids can go. He thinks he is getting a toothache. Probably the return of an abscess that he had twenty years ago. He is old. He will rest in the car. My sister wants to stay. No, no. He will be alright. He will watch the rain. He will see if he can see America.

The indecision is becoming unbearable. We have nursed him along so far – should we now take him at a word that he does not really mean? We both take the same decision, communicated in a glance. OK, we say, we will take you at your word. You stay here, we won't be long. And in moments we have gone. We are buying tickets. We are walking into the cliff in search of bears, leaving a bearish parent at the surface.

At first there is a light-heartedness about it. We kids are unbound. Having tended his every wish these last weeks we taste momentary freedom. But when we have come a long way, and an encouraging guide says we have done forty minutes and only have twenty to go, I remark that he would have found this long walk, and especially the return, very difficult. Then my hand, in a pocket, encounters the car keys. I had not meant to bring them. Did I lock the car? If he tries to get out will he set off the alarms? We are now in the cave.

The guide is showing us the bones of the bear's kill. I can hardly concentrate. Another thought strikes me. Did I put the handbrake on? It was very windy on that cliff top. We are in the front of the car park, with only an unsubstantial fence between the car, the cliffs and the Atlantic. *What if I had not applied the brake? What if the car rolled forward in the wind? What if another vehicle nudged ours from the rear? What if …?*

I shared my fears with my sister. I only got half of it out. She knew exactly what we should do – and ran back up the tunnel. Had we been pursued by the prehistoric bear himself we could not have gone faster.

When we at length reached the car park we were blown. The wind had dropped and the rain had ceased. The car was still there. As we ran towards it we could see that this sleeping bear was still in the same position. The car was locked. The handbrake was fully applied, the gear shift was in the reverse position. We sat down and sobbed with relief, rehearsing to each other how we would have explained things to our mother had our worst fears been justified. At this point the sleeper awoke. His toothache grumbled. He was hungry but doubted if he could eat anything. How far were we from the hotel? He needed whiskey, purely for medicinal purposes. What on earth was the matter with us? Stop giggling like idiots and drive to the hotel!

After dinner and a good deal more medicinal whiskey he retired to bed, but he was up early in the morning. It was a Sunday. That toothache was worse. We needed to find a dentist, or if none was available a sympathetic vet would do. I went to consult Mr O'Brien, the hotel manager. The nearest town was Ennis and he did not know that either would be available. The dentist to whom he usually sent hotel guests was away, having left to nurse her sick mother up in Westport for the weekend. It was a real puzzler as to how to help. He had no oil of cloves in the hotel. The pharmacies were all closed on a Sunday in Ennis, and this village was particularly quiet this Sunday. The church was locked, Mass now only being said here every other Sunday since the population had dropped so low...

Then, with a shout, he said, "I have it! Would you describe your Father as being a suggestible man? I mean, does he believe in ghosts, saints, miracles?"

"Well," I responded, "he certainly believes in Providence."

"So," said Mr O'Brien, "we must make him believe that Providence has provided. Our church here in the village is dedicated to St Tola of Clonard. Tola was a bishop over in Meath but around 700 he came over here and founded a monastery between the River Fergus and the Burren. No one knows where that was, but there is a shrine to him in the churchyard and a sacred spring bubbles out from beneath it."

I pointed out that fascinating local history as this was, a bear with a wound was rolling around in an upstairs bedroom.

"Ah, but what you do not know, Mr Worlock, is that Tola is

the patron saint of toothaches in Ireland. You can see his staff in the National Museum in Dublin. It's got a bit cut out which was where you put the tooth that needed attention. Now, my suggestion to you is that someone with credibility with your father, like your sister for instance, should tell him that water drawn from Tola's holy well, taken last thing at night and first thing in the morning is a sovereign cure. A certain specific for the job. And Providence has laid this in his way this Sunday with very deliberate intent. And tell him that it only works on people in a reasonable state of Grace. If he is hiding some great and unconfessed sin he should forget it."

I considered the options: there was only one. So I asked where I could find the spring.

"Well," said O'Brien, "get your sister pumping up the expectations first. Then I will give you an empty half carafe to take with you when you climb over the wall. It is important that your father appreciates the difficulties of bringing this cure back. Let your sister describe to him the arduous struggle, the height of the wall, your inevitable injuries, the thickets of sedge and reeds you had to battle through, the need to emulate St Tola by rescuing a damsel in distress, at length returning with the cure."

I passed the message on to Mary and set out on my pilgrim-age mission, slipping through the easy stile in the churchyard wall and down the well-weeded paths until I found the shrine and the spring. I filled the vessel. There was an elderly lady trimming a grave and on the way out she asked me for a hand over the stile. I passed her basket over to her but slipped in the mud on my side and lost my shoe. Fortunately no precious water was spilt and I was able to bring the full cargo back to the hotel.

When I returned I found my sister had been working well. Father looked at me as I handed over the water.

"Mary says this will work and she never lies," he said. "Had you come with such a story I would have laughed. You would say anything."

He obediently drank half of the contents of the carafe before retiring. The half-full carafe was put in a wall niche in the room already occupied by a plaster saint. It seemed right. He was up and about bright and early in the morning and said he had drunk the second half as soon as he got up.

"Do you feel better?"

"From what?"

"The toothache."

He shrugged. "Did I really have a toothache, last night? Thought I must have imagined it. At any rate, blessed Providence heard the prayers of my grandmother and great-aunt and interceded."

My sister and I exchanged a glance and at the check-out desk O'Brien winked broadly and pushed the church restoration fund donation box towards me. I paid our dues.

The journey to the airport was uneventful, and we were quiet and tired as I drove the car up from Heathrow to the Cotswolds. As we neared Evenlode, Father said, "It is as I have always maintained. A day spent five miles from your own front door is a day wasted."

My sister and I exchanged glances again. Triumphant glances. We had brought him back to my mother and his moorings substantially intact and unchanged. We felt vindicated – and very relieved.

Chapter 26

Rising and Falling

T HE ENGLISH FARMERS of Father's generation behaved
publicly as though they believed that social status
was fixed for ever, but acted privately as if it could be
changed in a generation. It was of huge importance to them.
Marriage, inheritance and bonanza (a building-stone quarry
on the Clark family farm, or a business park at Nibley) could
make all the difference between a tenant and a farmer who
owned his land, between a farmer who could apply fertiliser
at the right levels and one who was even more at the mercy of
soil and micro-climate by not being able to do so. One of the
reasons why Father and his peers observed each other's efforts
so closely was not just envy: they read in every crop who was

making it to a greater position of security, and who was at even greater risk than themselves of losing their balance on the agricultural log.

So when Father spoke of the Worlocks "crawling up a crack in the hills" to get to the Cotswold top country, he wasn't only making a contrast between the small scale of their farming down at Coombe, near Wotton, in the Severn Vale and the greater prosperity achieved at Tresham, on the edge of the escarpment, and at Calcot, on the top country itself. He wasn't only talking about a journey that took three hundred years but only travelled three miles. He was talking about a change in social positioning whose demarcations and definitions were so fine that only the participants, in the villages, could properly see them for what they were.

The Worlocks, for example, were never gentry. In my days as a student of history I appreciated that gentry were always rising and falling, according to whether you were reading R. H. Tawney or Christopher Hill or Lawrence Stone. Father's letters received always gave him the courtesy of "W. R. G. Worlock Esq" but this meant nothing. He hunted with dukes and earls but knew the boundaries too well to trespass. His generation was sure-footed in terms of English social distinctions. So just where were the Worlocks in social-class terms, and where did he think they were going? And why was it important that they were going anywhere?

In order to grip this we have to decode a great deal of intricate social stratification. Generally, it seemed that a farmer–landowner had greater status than a tenant, unless of course you were a tenant of a great landowner like the Duke of Beaufort: that carried status and security. But generally the farmer–owner was seen to be better placed than the tenant. Not necessarily wealthier, but with assets that could be mortgaged in hard times.

A tenant on a maintaining lease, having to keep the farmhouse and buildings in good repair, could suffer the worst of all worlds.

Then there was the difference between arable and the grazier. Down in the vale, while there was much fertile alluvial soil, there were also heavy clays, fields that had never been cultivated. (When we ploughed the water meadows at Evenlode one year they dried out – and blew away the next year, forcing us to try to recreate the rich ley that we had so wantonly destroyed.) The historical landholding patterns differed from vale to escarpment. Those small enclosed fields that grazed milking cows, steers and sheep in the vale gave way to field sizes ten times greater on the top country. The fertility per acre might be lower, but the average size of farms was much greater. Better by far to be at the top of the hill than the bottom. The Worlocks of Coombe, near Wotton, were a social notch below the Worlocks of Tresham and Ozleworth. They were none of them "gentlemen": the word carried connotations of owning land but not working it oneself. But even amongst yeoman farmers there were differences, and everyone knew them.

But who cared? Well, Gran, for one. She was a Hatherall from on top of the hill. Did she feel she had married beneath her status? Whenever she said "keep yourself up", I sensed her keen awareness of the importance of social positioning and the risk of downward sliding. For my mother this sense was also critical. Imbued by her mother-in-law with the importance of being on the top rung of the farmer ladder, she bloomed as a powerful presence in Evenlode society, somewhere between the minor titled gentry ("You know, when you get to speak to them they are really surprisingly quite like us!") and the tenant farmers. In those days you could invite "up" but not "down": though we loved Bert Harford and his wife, neighbours and tenant farmers at Nibley, we would never have invited them to dinner. While some of the more superficial snobbery of the English class system had by now departed, a good deal remained in place, and it pervaded every aspect of our lives.

A part of the journey up that crack in the hills was a journey from the chapel, in this case Baptist, to Church of England. This had little to do with religious faith and everything to do with social prominence. The box tombs at Ozleworth are a statement of Worlock social aspiration as much as the family graves at Tresham.

Father never lost his sense of deference. But he also never lost an underlying feeling that he was as good as any and better than most. He would rather sell a horse to a gentleman than to "someone who knew something about it". Since he was blessed with infinite curiosity, he was as regular a trespasser on foot or by car as on a horse. If my mother was present she would beg him to go back before we were seen and spare her the awful embarrassment of being discovered. If he had children with him he seemed more outrageous in his wanderings, almost as if they were human shields against the wrath of owners and occupants.

Going to see a horse accompanied by me, we found that the animal had been sold before we arrived. Sitting next to him in the Land Rover I feared an outbreak of bad temper, since these were the days in the mid 1950s when that was a fairly common occurrence. But we drove away quite calmly. After a mile or so, as if in an emergency or to avoid a collision, he turned the steering wheel sharply to the left. We went up a narrow drive, at the top of which was a gate. I was curtly told to get out and open it. I did, and just scrambled back in as we drove away. We were in parkland, approaching a wooded area, when he stopped and parked up beside a hedge.

"Now on foot," he said. "Coming?"

I knew there wasn't a realistic option, so I followed.

We went through another gate and then found ourselves coming down a slope into the back of some stable yards.

"They have some great horses here," he said. "This is Lyegrove House, home to the Earl and Countess of Westmoreland. Looks better from the front."

As he strode on I knew I was my mother's son. What would happen if we were caught? Would we be arrested? Would the police come? And then my worst fears were realised.

"I say," said a cultured voice. "Can I help you? Do you have business here? What do you want?"

We turned. The figure before us was very much a gentleman, from his cavalry twills right up to the leather patches on the elbows of his tweed jacket. Father cleared his throat, and began in a much richer and more intense Gloucestershire accent than normal.

"You see, sir, it's like this. I just come up here to satisfy the boy, he being so anxious to see and all …"

"See what?" said the man impatiently. "Spit it out. I have things to do."

"Well," says Father, now holding his hat in his hands and rotating the brim through his fingers in a convincing demonstration of shy, peasant anxiety. "It's your kitchens, you see …"

"Well, damned if I know what our kitchens mean to you …"

"Well, sir, if you just give us a moment to explain. The boy's grandmother, my mother, if you understand me. Well, she is always going on about your kitchens. She was in service here as a young woman and it made a great impression on her. So we come round this way, so as not to disturb anyone in the house, as you understand. Thought I might find Cook. Or someone who might give the boy a peak at where his gran worked. Not so as to cause any offence, you understand…"

There was a silence while all this was digested by the three of us. Father was obviously hearing it for the first time and was quite impressed. I was caught in two minds: what would Gran do to Father if she ever found this out was uppermost, but somewhere else I wondered how anyone could possibly believe such rubbish. And just as I was thinking that, our interrogator responded.

"Well, I am sure we can accommodate that. I like curiosity in a lad. We can get Bartlett or one of the under-butlers to show you round. I say, lad," now addressing me. "You'll be able to tell her how we have modernised things since her day. Did we have electricity then? Come along, let's get this organised."

And so we did. A young man appeared in striped trousers. A visit to the kitchen with its huge ranges was proffered and taken. Enough intelligent questions were asked to confirm the good intentions of the visitors. The boy was given a glass of lemonade and a piece of cake. The under-butler bade us a cheerful farewell, only commenting that if we ever wanted to come again we should probably phone up and make an appointment. We had to go down the main drive, and then cut back into the estate again to retrieve the Land Rover. It was a long walk but not a word was spoken.

When we were in the vehicle, Father said I should not talk of this in case it ever came to Gran's ears. He explained that while the little story had been necessary at the time for us, she would find it hurtful. I promised. But my own feelings were in turmoil. I sensed Father's feeling of triumph. I sensed that he felt he had been in a tricky place but had dodged a bullet. But I felt a bit chastened by the experience, a reluctant party to a lie, a prop on stage when the magician does a dramatic routine, and I got my first intimation of an element of the English class system which is as pervasive as its snobbery. While you may look down on those said to be below you in the social pecking order, those said to be below you are likely to view you as a chinless wonder whose credulity is there to be exploited.

We lived in a class-bound world at Nibley Farm in 1955, and for Father this remained a condition of life throughout his life. He had some of the inverted snobbery of our village postman at Evenlode, who once told me over a confidential pint in the British Legion club in Moreton-in-Marsh that he "could not stand or a-bear with 'new money'". The subject he was discussing at the time was Lord Dulverton, scion of W. D. & H. O. Wills' tobacco fortune and then owner of Batsford Park, whose family home it had been since the end of the First World War. For Father it was the title that mattered. He revered impoverished baronets of slender means as much as the earls and dukes with whom he crossed paths out hunting.

"It's breeding, Dave."

Gran alluded to the Worlocks as having "good blood", and hinted at illicit trysts and even relationships producing offspring, with noble families in the hills.

Father was dismissive. "Two glasses of sherry and she will rewrite the family tree."

As a teenager I thought it all too possible: at the age when you wonder how you could possibly have been born into a family like this, the thought that I might be the great-great-grandson of a ducal bastard was quite appealing.

But in the microcosm of Nibley Farm in 1955 the class stratification was all too clear. And Father was at the top of it. The men who worked for him expected him to know what he was doing, but respected his right to be eccentric, a right he exercised to the full. The fact that he would be away hunting at times when they might want decisions never appeared to trouble anyone. The senior man, at first Bob Williams and later

Ben (Paul Benjamin), were quite capable of making the petty decisions and the rest could wait. Ben in his time had the use of a farm cottage, and effectively managed the vital milking herd. Below him in rank and estimation were the weekly paid farm labourers like Chris and Gerald, and then the harvest and threshing day labourers, the apprenticeship boys who had to have a year of farmwork experience before going to agricultural college and finally, until his demise, Fred Timbrell. Father did not believe that farm cottages should ever be repossessed. Mrs Dando lived in hers, on the strength of her late husband's work on the farm, until her death, and so did Fred. Of the four cottages attached to the farm and intended for farm workers, two were occupied by pensioners.

Elsewhere, the village was the pub, the shop, and the mill, plus about twenty-five houses. Behind the pub was a smallholding, comprising a barn and two fields, with a third tucked away behind the mill on the Iron Acton road. In short, this was a microcosm of class in Britain in 1955, and we were all acutely aware of it. Every time Mrs Dando called me "Master David" I was reminded that the big house in the village was the farmhouse and that, in the tiny domain of the village, Father was the lord of the manor. The respectful attitudes of his farm labourers (to his face, at least) underlined this. Yet in a bigger world Father was well aware of his place, and he had the whole post-feudal social structure of "Beaufortshire" around him to remind him, should he be in doubt for a moment. His universal condemnation, like the Evenlode postman, was for "new money", especially if he thought it had been used for flashy or ostentatious show. Yet he never for a moment hesitated about taking the money off such people.

When we arrived at Evenlode and began to tackle its gardens, he was annoyed by the severe scorching of the bark of a lone spruce tree in the yard. Walking past it every day he came to see the tree as a mast, and before long, using Cotswold drystone walling for its hull, he had built a boat for that mast, thus disguising the burn scars and providing an additional flower bed.

But when a neighbour, one whose income did not derive from the soil, improved the approach to his house by removing the dilapidated wooden farm gate and replacing it with stone pillars, topped with eagles, and wrought iron gates hung between them, he spoke of outrage. This was a pretence at a position in society that had not been earned. The corollary of knowing your position in society was knowing your place, and if you did try to improve it, as the Worlocks did on their long voyage up the valley from Coombe to Tresham, this had to be an imperceptible, multi-generational rise recognised by and acceptable to the rest of the community. Social mobility was permissible, but in a society locked to the land for survival and dependent, as it thought, on male succession for continuity, knowing your position and place as well as that of the whole community were vital features in a class driven world.

Chapter 27

Conclusion

THE BUREAU STANDS in the corner of my study, just as it has stood in a Worlock place of business for the past hundred and seventy years or so. In my great-grandfather's day it was used to store the farm accounts. It held the strongbox. Here the wages were made up and here the men were paid and signed the ledger. Here I have watched my mother "making up the money" and here I have watched Father handing it out on Saturday mornings, always benign and with kind enquiries for the children, siblings or parents of the recipients. These relationships were poorly paid, but they were not just wage relationships.

I do not write at the bureau anymore, using its broad frontal flap, supported by two pull-out wooden rods. From the move to Evenlode onwards I have worked and written at Gran's desk. It's a little small and the drawers have warped, but although I work mostly at a keyboard, I like to look at the onyx inkwell stand, with two pots divided by a miniature stag's head and antlers, and every month I move time onwards on her silver-mounted perpetual universal calendar which, since she received it as a wedding present, has moved Worlock months forward for around a hundred and thirty years.

And this in itself has been but a passing moment in the long history of the Worlocks, Wherlocks, Werlocs, Warlocks or wherever spelling fashions next take us. Were we the oath breakers of legend ("Waer-logga") that associates witches with us? Or, as some historians claim, were we in fact oath-makers, notarising oaths and witnessing agreements. Ironically, on the wall opposite me as I write is an agreement of 1819 notarised by one "John Worlock". Did the tradition live on? What seems fairly certain after this Anglo-Saxon etymological confusion is that a family of Saxon and Viking intermarriage became settled farmers in the Midlands and East Anglia. From the thirteenth century they begin to appear in rent rolls and land records, as tenants and villeins, even as serfs, but never as landlords.

This is the context in which what I have written should be read. Survival and succession had served them well for five hundred years before my story begins. It was not an unreasonable expectation that it would go on serving them well. In their own times, the two generations before mine had come through two world wars, severe agricultural depressions, agricultural depopulation in the villages, pandemics that robbed them of people like my grandfather – and who was to say that these things would not continue, or are not continuing now? So, surely, people who said "stick to the tried and tested formula" cannot be said to be unreasonable.

Time has passed. I see the things I fought for and about as a boy and young man in a different perspective. Father, with little good and pleasurable experience of his own father, and driven by his mother's determination to keep her family afloat, acted out in my childhood his received impression of how fathers treated and prepared and hardened their sons for the battle for agricultural survival ahead. Father, in an endless tension with his mother and his wife who saw all the economic difficulties so clearly, knew he could only survive if he could preserve the core of his existence – his horses and his hunting. These things, which could never be afforded, and on which time spent was seen by many as time wasted which should have been dedicated to the land, had become essential expressions of himself in the years between his father's death and the marriage that gave him reassurance and support for the rest of his life.

He was a richly eccentric character, and that was there before the sale of Nibley Farm. It became more marked afterwards as he became financially secure for the first time in his life. Once our relationship re-established itself we never spoke again about the conflict over whether I should be a farmer. Ten years before Father's death in 1996 I had the impertinence to suggest he might think about some estate planning, and brought my own financial advisers down to the farm to talk to him.

After a pleasant lunch he laughingly sent them away with the words, "What's mine is mine, and you never know what happens next. When we go, the kids will have it all and I won't be worried about the taxes!"

But my mother did give me his will, told me I was the executor and asked me to "bring it up to date". I soon saw what she meant. The will granted me an option, should I decide to farm the land, to buy out my sisters on very favourable terms over a long period of years. We soon rewrote this on the basis of equal terms for all, but it reflects the idea that a dim glimmer of my possible return was not extinguished until he really didn't care about it at all.

A close companionship lasted until I had him no more. He died in 1996 while I was in New York on business (I was staying in the old Carlyle Hotel, and asked them to get me on the first flight out: he would have appreciated the elderly reception clerks with their card index systems for recording client preferences. Next time I stayed there the clerk solemnly informed me that he was giving me the room in which my father had died).

After the funeral I was often at the farm, comforting my mother and clearing up bits of family business. Sometimes I would get the Land Rover out and drive slowly round to Great Wolford or Bourton, places where he exercised horses every day, and often shared a companionable pint with me. And in those early weeks the landlord would commiserate and say how much they all missed him.

And then a pause.

"...And of course he never had any money...Times I've served him, sittin' outside on that gert hoss of his ... Still, he always said I could rely on you bein' round ...There is the matter of this small bar bill..."

He spoke often in his last years of the changes he had seen: we are all prone to this. He thought hunting would not survive him, not because of the pressure to ban cruel sports but because of the intensity of farming. The farm of his youth was in every way horse-drawn. He saw the dawn of mechanisation. Our first tractor came with Lend-Lease. Electricity replaced the oil and kerosene lamps.

When he was in this mood I would remind him of a day when he was broadcasting rape seed. We used a bag of seed slung round his neck in which, through two metal rings in the sides, was passed a "bow" like a violin bow. Drawing the bow to and fro caused seed to arc out on either side as he strode down the field. But he was worried that no seed fell behind him. So I was pressed into service with a bucket of seed to walk in his footsteps and scatter it as I went. Having checked the wind direction, a factor that could ruin everything, off we set, in a scene reminiscent of the Late Middle Ages. I can recall how hard it was to keep up, and the imprecations that followed if he found me lagging.

But I remember too the Fordson tractor, and I have, as described above, worked with a horse hoe. I recall the storage heaters that made rooms warm where our blazing fires simply created hot spots and icy corners. I had laid hedges and built Cotswold stone walls without a hint of cement. I was the first person in my family to go to university. I became a publisher on the simple principle that I wanted to spend my life doing something that I would want to do even if no one paid me (though I kept this thought secure from my employers). In time and in the 1980s I was swept onwards from books and education into the world of digital information, fortunate at each stage to find teachers who would introduce new concepts and patiently explain to me what they meant.

Yet I may not have travelled further than Father, or travelled at all. Some years ago, in a coach between Agra and Delhi, I glanced out at the parched and dusty plains of northern India and saw an Indian farmer broadcasting seeds, followed by his son, with a bowl, covering his footsteps.

Lightning Source UK Ltd.
Milton Keynes UK
UKHW012022290421
382855UK00001B/58